THE POWER OF
MOVING
THE
MIDDLE

Transforming your middle performers into high achievers

JACK SPARTZ

All comments and direct quotes are the writer's interpretation of speeches, presentations, discussions, and/or written material.

The Power of Moving the Middle
Transforming your middle performers into high achievers
Published by Jack Spartz

Cover design and editing by Henderson Shapiro Peck.

Printed in the United States of America.

For more information, visit: WWW.JACKSPARTZ.COM

 Dedication

To my Mom, Dad, and my little brother Richard, our guardian angel.
You will always be in my heart, and I miss you very much.

Forward

Abraham Lincoln is purported to have said that "The Lord prefers common people. That is why he made so many of them." Mr. Lincoln's point supports the theme of this book: how can we design a system to help ordinary individuals perform better than even they believe possible? Or more specifically in the business world, how can a company improve its performance by Moving the Middle? This question is critical to our success because the middle forms the bulk of our workforce.

As you will quickly learn as you read the book, Jack Spartz is not only a business strategist but also an Ironman athlete. I first met Jack in 2005 while cycling in the north Georgia mountains. The climbs take anywhere from 30 minutes to an hour per mountain which gives you ample time to get to know each other's character and stories. In the ensuing ten years, Jack and I trained together for countless Ironman races and probably rode over 50,000 miles together.

During those hours on the bike I had the pleasure of listening, analyzing and debating Jack's theories on performance. Jack is an avid reader and believed what he was reading in books like *Boys in the Boat* was present in all human beings, it just needed the right environment, motivation, and leadership to bring it to life. Through his studies, research, and profession, Jack has dedicated himself to unlocking this secret of performance.

What's even more exciting is that I have also had the pleasure of watching Jack's theory in action with the Five Star program he developed for the largest telecommunications company in the country. Five Star was designed to Move the Middle performers by improving their efficiency, quality, productivity, safety, and customer satisfaction. The program focused not only on the Top Performers who almost always do well, but also the Middle Performers who had been performing well below potential. Our finance team tracked, measured, and confirmed the improvements in all the key areas of the program.

Jack, through his experience, realized that cash incentives were not the best means for motivating middle performers – so he built the program leveraging recognition, personal improvement goals, and a point-based reward system similar to the airline frequent flyer programs. Earning and accumulating points enabled team members to demonstrate their accomplishments with incredible awards and with meaningful recognition from their leaders and peers. Five Star touched people in a very personal way. One technician, who passed away from an unfortunate off the job accident, was so proud of his Five Star designation that his family buried him with his Five Star hat. From this experience and many others, we knew Five Star and Jack's approach to Moving the Middle was positively changing our culture.

As you read the book, you will quickly understand that Jack is an outstanding and accomplished individual. His book captures his can-do spirit and vision for inspiring Lincoln's "common people." He weaves personal stories throughout the book to illustrate the principles and secrets he has unlocked, which makes for eminently enjoyable reading. The book will also give you a sense of some of those long discussions climbing and descending the beautiful Appalachian mountains.

William W. Hague
(Formerly) Executive Vice President
Global Connections Management

TABLE OF CONTENTS

This book was written to change the way you think about solving your greatest challenge: your middle performers. As you'll learn from the stories and principles in the book, the problem of subpar performance isn't an issue with your people, it's with your managers, your environment, your culture, and you. To successfully change a company, you have to understand the social influences that helped create the problems you face.

Moving the Middle was a term created and used in business that refers to improving the performance of what many would consider average performers. In truth there are no average performers, just employees, students, and teams that have either lost their drive, motivation, or desire to deliver more than their current performance level.

The Middle is safe, it's comfortable and it's your biggest opportunity to improve the performance of your team, company, and service to your clients. You as a company will spend millions on new technology, products, marketing, and real estate to provide the best possible experience and services for your customers, but if your employees are complacent you've missed the most important key to your success: their drive, creativity, energy, commitment, and sense of pride.

The principles that we'll discuss in this book apply to our personal lives as well as our corporate environments. Most people desire to change, to improve, and to realize their potential. As in everything in life, that's easier said than done. It's difficult to follow through and do it.

I wrote this book because through the course of a lifetime of reading, researching, and testing hundreds of theories on improving performance, I realized that something very important was missing: how to move the middle performers. If emotionally engaged, those individuals could deliver billions of dollars in productivity, growth, and profitability.

Shannon Thompson recently wrote that "one of the most enjoyable aspects of working as a specialist in any field is the opportunity to learn and experiment with new strategies." I know that joy, and I loved where the journey took me and the lessons it taught me.

Most of the top selling books are focused on top performers, good to great, peak performance, and the heart and mind of winners. Where are the books, the stories, or even the principles of how to tap into the biggest opportunity facing American businesses today? How can we move the middle performers? Any idea of what the value of moving the middle is worth if you can improve it just 1% in your company? How about in your industry? How about 5%? How about just one metric like quality or customer retention? You should know— and you should know where those improvements can make the biggest impact on your business and performance.

I am an architect, a strategist, and a pragmatic business leader. What you're going to learn from this book came from a life of collaboration, of designing and implementing performance improvement and change management programs.

As a result of my experiences, I became good at understanding what drives human behavior in the work place and made a career of creating initiatives that change the culture and the performance of teams. Over sixteen years, I leveraged this knowledge and experience into building some of the most successful change management initiatives of their kind in the world.

Through the process of testing, refining, and implementing new initiatives I refined my team's approach and made an art and science of the discipline of Moving the Middle. My team knew where to start, what to ask, the data to analyze and the way to lead the process. We knew how to assess our successes and failures and how, when and where to adjust our designs to maintain the momentum, dynamic tension and interest to sustain performance over an indefinite period of time.

<u>When we designed and implemented new initiatives, we knew our success was predicated on changing deeply-rooted cultures and long-held beliefs and behaviors to improve results.</u>

Over the years we developed unique, proven, and scalable processes across multiple industries, roles, and job functions. In the process we changed businesses and lives.

Many of the key lessons I discovered through my experiences were in stark contrast to what leaders have proclaimed as the path to greatness. Success is not easy, and if you're not disciplined, creative, and highly iterative in your approach, chances are you'll begin backsliding before you realize it. Throughout the book I share stories of what we did, how we did it, and our results with the hope that you'll try some of the approaches and, through those experiences, achieve greater awareness and success.

There's an old saying that "if you give a manager enough money, he can solve any problem." I do not subscribe to that belief. I have watched leader after leader try to solve performance problems with cash, and although they may close a short-term gap, the strategy never solves a performance issue.

Chances are you picked up this book because you're struggling with making your numbers, closing a performance gap, or deciding if you have a leadership or employee problem. At no point should you expect everyone on your team to become top performers, but you should expect you and your managers to be leading high-performing teams. That is an important distinction as you begin to understand how you can change the middle and the performance of your company.

The stories and examples in the book are based on my experience in creating and implementing programs designed to improve the performance of over 100,000 employees and managers ranging from sales reps to customer service reps and service technicians.

The initiatives referenced in the book supported one of the largest telecom companies on the planet with one of the initiatives generating savings of over $500 million dollars over eight years. We achieved these results through productivity, quality, efficiency, safety, and customer satisfaction improvements.

On a separate initiative, the client generated over $500 million in incremental sales revenue from an employee referral program. **That's a billion dollar+ impact with just one company.** The most incredible part of the experience was that the initiatives evolved and scaled to impact other areas of the business we never imagined.

We designed a number of other client initiatives using the principles of Moving the Middle. What all the programs demonstrated was that employees in the middle, when inspired and properly motivated, can and will improve their performance.

Every concept we explored was piloted so we had data to compare the control group to the pilot group. There was no denying the behavioral as well as the financial impact we were making before we scaled to other teams, groups, and divisions. The pilots and initiatives taught us one of the most important lessons that we all need to understand: that to get employees to improve their performance was less about their compensation and more about their sense of connection, contribution, and progress.

That was an important revelation because it meant that we could achieve our goals without dramatically changing their existing compensation structure.

The single most impressive financial result from one of our key initiatives was that over **90% of the costs savings came from the middle performers.** Contrary to expectations, moving the middle performers offered the best investment from an impact and ROI perspective.

What made these experiences so rewarding was that my team and I had the opportunity to create positive change in one the most challenging business environments: union-based work groups. If you think your work group is tough, try getting unions to approve even a raise hike without years of negotiations and the possibility of strikes. That's exactly what we did.

The differences between the artist, the craftsman, and the amateur are the knowledge, experience, and ability in which they're capable of shaping an outcome. This book will make you more cognizant of these elements, but your own designs and pilots will determine where you end up on the spectrum between artist and amateur.

As you read the book you'll notice that the book's most important concepts and tools are underlined, forcing your brain to pause, think, and re-read the passage.

These same underlined points are summarized at the back of the book in the final chapter, so you can have a quick reference guide to the most important concepts in the book.

 Bottom line: The greatest gains in successful initiatives were not driven by top performers, but getting and keeping the middle performers emotionally engaged. The greatest value for improvement is in Moving the Middle.

Moving the Middle changes performance and cultures.

✓ The greatest untapped value in your business is grounded in Moving the Middle.

✓ Moving the Middle promotes Aspirational and Emotional Commitment.

✓ It communicates expectations and recognizes individual and team performance consistently and meaningfully.

✓ It is visible at all levels of the organization because it's aligned with leadership imperatives.

✓ It creates an emotional connection to a purpose that is part of something bigger and greater than individual performance.

✓ It fuels engagement, performance and helps create a culture of recognition.

✓ Recognizing your people consistently and with meaning increases your ability to reinforce key messages and aligns the needs of the business with recognition and performance.

CHAPTER 1

THE MIND
OF THE
MIDDLE

"The mind creates
its own reality."

– Mind Power, John Kehoe

Born in the Middle

My parents were incredible role models, and my dad was my hero. He played college football for Creighton University and earned the rank of Captain in the Marines while serving the country during World War II. Stationed in the Pacific Theater as a Bomb Disposal Officer, he was awarded three Bronze Stars. After the war he met my mom, had 12 children, and became a successful father, husband, and salesman. I'm sure if they'd had 2 or 3 kids, life would have been very different but not necessarily better. I was number eight of the twelve and became famous for always telling everyone I was my parents' favorite.

The age difference between the oldest and youngest was 18 years.

My earliest memories are from our 3-bedroom bungalow in Cicero, a suburb of Chicago. There was a tavern at the end of our block, and during the summers we used to play fastpitch baseball in the parking lot behind the tavern. Remember that scene from The Sandlot with kids hitting balls into the yard with the dog? Our neighborhood's dog's name was King and to this day I have an intense fear of German Shepherds.

We lived in that house with 10 children and 2 parents for 6 years. There were 2 rooms for the kids. One for the sisters and one for the brothers. We didn't think we were poor; we thought we were normal. We had it so good as kids that we were actually featured in an article by Jack Mabley, a well-known newspaper reporter in Chicago. The title of the article was *Huck Finn Never Had It So Good!*

The middle has always been my life. As the eighth of twelve kids growing up in a middle class working family, I was a middle performer in school, work, and sports. I was good at the middle. I knew how to just get by and shield my disappointment from my siblings, friends, and parents by making jokes about my less than stellar results and outcomes.

Let's face it— being in the middle undermines your belief and confidence in yourself. Your behavior begins to reinforce those beliefs and eventually you slide from the middle to the bottom without even knowing it. My grades said I was a middle performer, my teachers treated me like a middle performer and because there were no books on how to inspire, teach, or engage middle performers I got stuck in the middle.

Despite being six foot five, I wasn't much better than average in basketball, golf, or any other sport I played. My mom used to refer to my coordination as that of a baby deer. How embarrassing! After college I became a swimmer, runner, and cyclist, but in 5k road races to the Ironman distance triathlon, I've always ranked comfortably in the middle. You might read Ironman and be thinking "middle performer?" Yes— I was very much in the middle, even as an athlete pursuing a goal like an Ironman triathlon.

I competed in triathlons for over twenty years before getting the courage to sign up for an Ironman. Once I got a taste of the Ironman and what it felt like to cross the finish line and wear the Ironman logo, I went on to start nine more Ironman races and finish five. My reason for sharing the Ironman experience is that I've found there are a number of parallels from endurance sports, personal achievement, and business that I believe help illustrate the principles of Moving the Middle.

My results say I'm a middle performer, but that's not who I am and that's not who you are or who you have on your team. Some of my greatest insights about Moving the Middle came from what I learned from the "endurance community" that was embracing average people and getting them to do extraordinary things.

The "endurance community" taught me about motivation, goals, perseverance, social influences, consistency, recognition, reinforcement, and changing performance. I weave these principles and stories throughout the book so you can better understand their implications in your strategies and designs.

After graduating from college, I realized that my love of reading could expand and accelerate my education – that reading could take me into areas that I had never explored in school. I read every book I could get my hands on in the areas of business, personal biographies, behavior, habits, and psychology. After years of just reading anything and everything, I noticed that a few months after reading a book, I couldn't remember the key points or facts from them. Frustrated at the obvious waste of time, I began the process of underlining key passages in books and then copying them into my 5" x 8" notebook.

This one extra step allowed me not only to have an incredible recall on principles, data, and research but by reviewing the material over time

<u>it helped me improve my understanding of experiences and events.</u> By adopting this discipline, I noticed that many of the authors weren't doers but researchers and writers.

What I quickly began to understand was that all we were being fed was "after the fact research" on a subject that many of the writers had never lived. I believed that if I was to improve and learn my profession, I needed to truly understand the people that had lived the experience, not just gloss over the writing of someone good at telling stories.

My notebook contains excerpts from an eclectic group of books and authors with such amazing insights that twenty years after starting the habit, it's still a discipline and resource I return to for grounding and advice. The authors in my notebook have seen me through my lowest career moments and guided me to my greatest career achievements.

<u>If you're looking for a way to get smarter faster, start writing things down in a notebook and review it every few days. The physical process of writing things down crystallizes thoughts, strengthens your neural pathways, and helps you learn it, understand it, and make it your own.</u> Your recall of important information will be dramatically improved as a result of this one discipline.

I hope as a result of reading this book you'll start your own notebook and incorporate some of the stories and principles from this book to inspire, teach, and provide guidance as you transform your team and your life. My goal in writing this book is simply to enrich the lives of others by sharing my experiences in a way that challenges you to think differently.

I've been asked why I'm not writing a book on the top performers and great leaders from my experiences. My answer is simply that <u>success is an illusion.</u> The team on top today struggles tomorrow. The player that carries his team to the championship today is tomorrow's headline for his problems and failures. The great performances of our time typically focus the lens on an individual when it's typically a team effort that made it happen.

Life is full of memorable stories of great individuals, coaches, and companies that crumbled under the pressure of the real world and expectations. We see it in sports, business, and personal lives. No, this isn't a story about those people. This is the story of the leaders and managers that defy the odds, create a culture of continuous improvement and achievement, and sustain their performance over long periods of time.

<u>One of the keys to sustained success is baked in the principles of your employee's aspirational desire to do something extraordinary and be a part of a winning team or meaningful purpose.</u> Creating that desire is what the great coaches do better than good managers. Wanting to do something versus having to do something changes the experience and shifts the culture from compliance to mission-driven.

If you're scratching your head wondering how successful companies and teams create mission driven cultures, just pick up the phone and order a pair of running shoes from Zappos. They built an entire culture on the aspirational desire to WOW! their customers and give their people the opportunity to go the extra mile to exceed customer expectations. As a result, Zappos is a recognized leader in not only customer satisfaction but employee productivity, engagement, and retention.

 <u>Bottom line:</u> Success is an illusion. It's a snapshot of a brief moment in time. The great leaders and coaches focus on creating cultures of continuous improvement and achievement and sustain their performance over long periods of time.

Life in the Middle

My first work experience was caddying at the Oak Park Country Club with my brothers. Caddying became a family tradition and our first exposure to the top financial producers and performers in the city. The people we caddied for were dentists, doctors, lawyers, bankers, successful business men, and their wives. We caddied for Olympians, pro football players, pro hockey players, and even professional entertainers.

My older brothers Tom, Bill, and Mike all worked for years as caddies with reputations as some of the best at the country club. They were, by definition, top performers. They ate, drank, and slept caddying. Every night they talked about the members, the caddies, and the funny things that happened that day.

Having never caddied but having heard all the stories, I couldn't wait to turn 13 and get started. The only problem was that it sounded easier than it was. Carrying bags that weighed 50–80 pounds for four hours was no small task for a skinny 13-year-old kid. Not losing golf balls, knowing the distances, and something as simple as raking the traps and tending the flag properly were challenging.

My first time caddying I earned $4.25. The flat rate was $4.00, and I earned a .25 tip for carrying my golfer's massive golf bag for 4 hours. Not the big money-making opportunity I thought it would be, but like most jobs I was probably paid what I was worth. Even in 1973 a dollar an hour was well below minimum wage, but it was the start of something special that I knew would change my life. We laughed about that quarter tip for years but we now laugh even harder at the golfer that gave me that tip.

Each year the members hosted a very high-end golf event at the country club. They spent thousands of dollars to participate in the "Invitational" which was a member-guest tournament. It was a 3-day event and was a chance for the club and members to entertain clients, friends, and future members. Big acts would be booked for the entertainment, and members celebrated all night and played dice and cards until dawn (always the highlight of the morning conversations).

In my first-year caddying at the event, I was assigned a member that must not have been very good because he got me as his caddy. I was average at best as a caddy and mostly went out with members that didn't want to pay for an experienced caddy.

On the second day of the golf tournament I was on the 18th green and tending the flag and my golfer hit a putt from 40 feet away. As I watched the ball come towards the hole, I froze. It looked like the perfect putt and was on track for going in until all the other golfers and caddies yelled at me to take out the flag. Too late. I didn't get the flag out in time, and the ball hit the pin and careened 10 feet in the opposite direction.

The golfer was visibly upset because he was then assessed a 2-shot penalty and still had to putt the ball in the hole to finish out the round. To make matters worse, the event happened right near the club's grill and pool where the members and guests were watching the last groups finishing up their rounds.

It may have been my lowest point of my life. I was in tears crying my heart out as one of the golfers, Mr. Gleason, put an arm around me, calmed me down and explained that despite what had happened, I wouldn't be fired and that everything would be ok. He knew I was giving the job my best, and all I needed was experience and encouragement to transform my performance.

Mr. Gleason was a successful banker and a father of eight kids who knew of me because of my older brothers. My guess is that after the round he met with my boss, the caddy master, and explained what happened and that it was an honest mistake that could have happened to any of the caddies.

Had Mr. Gleason not been on the green and in the foursome that day, my life could have ended up very differently. I could have been fired, and all the subsequent life experiences connected to caddying would have never happened. The fact that I still remember this experience like it was yesterday says a lot about Mr. Gleason, setbacks, coaching people up, and the importance of perspective.

Unlike me, my brother Mike was possibly the best caddy at the club. He was smart, curious, hardworking, and had mastered his understanding of the course. He didn't just tell you yardage, he told you how the wind would impact the shot and he read the greens. He told you where the pin was and where you wanted to play your shot to either play conservatively or aggressively. After watching the golfer play a few holes Mike told the golfer what club he thought they should hit and how they should play the shot.

When the golfers heard about my mistake I'm sure no one wanted me on their bag, which was why most of my loops (rounds of golf) that first year were with below-average golfers. I also got to caddy for the ladies and had a crush on more than a few of them. For most caddies, having to loop for the ladies was worse than not getting out, but for me it gave me a chance to develop my knowledge and experience of caddying— and the ladies were way more fun.

That summer my older brother Tom, who was a senior in high school, found out he won the Chick Evans Scholarship to Indiana University for caddying.

That Fall, we went down to Indiana University to visit Tom and to see a college for the first time. That trip changed my life. I came back aspiring to follow in Tom's footsteps, win the Chick Evans Scholarship, and go to Indiana University. Nothing else was ever the same after that event and once I made that commitment to myself.

The qualifications for earning the Chick Evans Scholarship rewarded not only excellence in school but hard work and effort. The candidate had to caddy for a minimum of 2 years, demonstrate financial need, rank in the top percentage of their graduating class, and get recommendations from the members at the country club.

The next year, my abilities as a caddy improved with experience, and I had something that not many other kids had at the time: emotional commitment to a goal. The key word was emotional. I didn't care about money, hanging out with my buddies, or playing high school sports. I was locked into one goal that I felt could change my life for the better: college!

No kid worked harder or more hours than I did for the next four years. If I was going to win that scholarship, I needed to stand out. In that country club, nothing stood out more than your rank as a caddy. To be number one was all about pride, recognition, and hustle. Despite being great caddies, none of my brothers had ever achieved number one status.

The grading system for caddies was simple and brilliant. After every round of golf, caddies were rated by golfers based on their performance. I wasn't anywhere near as good as the older caddies or my brother Mike, but six days a week I was there before the course opened and long after it closed.

Every few weeks, the list of the top 50 caddies was posted on the front window of the caddy shack. Based on the members' rating of their caddies after each round, the caddies earned five points for excellent, three for good, one for fair, and a negative five points for a poor rating. Every loop, job, or round moved me closer to my goal of going to college at Indiana University.

I didn't appreciate it at the time, but as I look back now, I better understand that it was my boss, the caddy master Bill Survilla, who helped me realize that goal. He could have fired me when he heard what happened on the 18th green during the invitational, but he used the experience to help motivate me to be my best.

Fortunately for me he appreciated my attitude, work ethic, and dream and decided to reinforce the effort knowing the skills and experience would come with time. Thanks to Bill and many others who supported my goal I finished that summer as the number one caddy in the club, outranking my brother Mike, who took second place.

It wasn't money I was after that summer, but the meaning, purpose, and goal of going to college that ignited my desire to excel. It didn't matter that I was average in ability. What mattered was that I believed I could get better and my boss reinforced that it was possible to achieve my goal. <u>The middle wasn't an obstacle. It was a benefit because I learned lessons and established abilities that would have otherwise remained dormant.</u>

Three years later, true to my vision and goal, I won the Chick Evans Scholarship, a four-year full ride scholarship to Indiana University.

Caddies at the Oak Park Country Club getting ready to caddy in the Evans Scholar Alumni Tournament.

The beauty of my experience was that growing up I was surrounded by great kids who had the same dream and worked just as hard caddying to earn the Scholarship. They didn't let the fact that they were raised in challenged financial situations hold them back. To the contrary, they used it as their motivation, and as a result developed a drive and discipline that helped them become doctors, lawyers, CFOs, and CIOs.

The key lesson about personal transformations and Moving the Middle isn't about skills or talent but hustle and effort. More times than not it's not a lack of skills that hold people back but their lack of desire to want to move forward.

As you read the book, you'll see that I'm purposely sharing real life experiences that are littered with the principles for one reason: you'll remember them. It would be easier to give you a bunch of business terms and models, but you won't remember any of them in a matter of months without an example of how to apply them.

What I do know from my own experience and research is that you'll remember the caddy pulling out the pin too late and Mr. Gleason's understanding and encouragement. You'll remember the goal of winning a college scholarship and the transformation that was required to get there. And you'll remember the caddy master Bill who helped me reach my goal by fueling my belief in myself.

Now I want you to think about just one person on your team for whom you could do what Bill did for me. <u>Lock in on that individual and hold on to that thought because as we build your plan and roadmap, it all comes down to creating the experience, one person at a time, that transforms your team and elevates your performance.</u>

I want this book to challenge you and help you think differently about your teams, employees, and possibly your kids, too. Who are those middle performers on your team who just need a little bit of encouragement to help ignite their desire?

After 15 years of evaluating corporate performance issues, one of the biggest blind spots I experienced was a leadership bias that ignored these middle performers and designed development strategies around the top performers. To create a winning team, you must re-engineer the way you think about this critical group of people and develop strategies for engaging all levels of the organization.

Middle Challenge questions...

✓ Ask your middle performers to define their motivation beyond the paycheck.

✓ Ask why that motivation is important to them.

✓ Ask them when they feel their greatest sense of commitment and purpose.

✓ The better you understand their motivation the more effective you'll be in designing initiatives that connect with their goals and purpose.

✓ Start simple and build on your successes and learn from your failures. Consistency and repetition are the key.

Bottom Line: The key lesson about personal transformations and moving the middle isn't about skills or talent but hustle and effort. More times than not it's not a lack of skills that hold people back but their lack of desire to want to move forward.

Small Wins

When I finished my first Ironman, I felt like Jimmy Valvano, the coach of North Carolina State University, running around the court looking for someone to hug after winning the NCAA men's basketball tournament.

I had worked hard, had a great race, and was ecstatic at finishing the hardest single-day race in sport!

My best friends had finished earlier and had already returned to their hotels. I laid in the med tent with my medal and finisher shirt getting an IV and thinking, "best day ever!"

After the race I was dehydrated, my throat was raw, I couldn't drink, and to eat was a pain worse than anything I'd ever experienced. It was such a long day.

After collecting my bike and bags full of racing shoes and clothes, I went back to my hotel and tried to get some sleep. No luck.

I was wired from all the Coke I'd drunk on the course, and at about 11:30 pm, I got up and walked over to the Waffle House down the street from the race finish. It was late, but the Waffle House was crowded with spectators and athletes just completing the race. It was then past midnight, but the energy in the place felt more like a college bar.

I found a seat over in the corner, and a few minutes later, two guys who had to weigh well over 300 pounds walked in and sat right behind me. One of them had an Ironman medal around his neck.

I spun around and said, "Congrats, how did your day go?"

The athlete with the medal thanked me and said he had an awesome race. He had a PR. A PR is a personal record and something triathletes like to mention when comparing their race times to previous efforts. Improving your time is always impressive no matter the course or conditions.

I asked the athlete what his finishing time was and he said 16:57 with a smile. I did a double take knowing the course closes officially at midnight, which is 17 hours after it opens. I asked, "this wasn't your first Ironman, but it was a PR. What may I ask was your other race time?"

He proudly responded, "16:59." A PR of 2 minutes! Small wins created feedback loops that reinforced the activities, behaviors, and habits that had inspired him to keep going.

The most interesting part of the story was the subsequent conversation with his friend who announced he was going to sign up for an Ironman. When asked if he was a runner or cyclist, he noted that he couldn't swim, but neither could his friend before he signed up for his first race, and look what he had just accomplished.

Is that an extreme case? Yes!

The world, Ironman, your company, and your team are full of untapped potential just waiting to be inspired to sign up and do something amazing with their life.

Most leaders don't have any idea how critical winning, desire, and motivation are to sustained success. If, after a period of attempts over time, your people don't experience success, they will lower their expectations or completely stop trying. They don't feel bad about being in the middle because the middle creates a culture all its own.

The middle performers reinforce the comfort of the middle by celebrating just showing up, not making waves, and making it through another week, not growth and improvement.

Listen to what is important to the middle:
1. It's not about being the best, but meeting expectations.
2. It's not about winning, but surviving.
3. It's not about delighting the customer, but following the company policies and procedures even when they know it's not right and doesn't measure up to your customer expectations.
4. "Doing my best" is their defense and a lie when they know their personal best is much better than what they are delivering.

Is there anything in a corporate environment that we can do to change this behavior?

Experience taught us that building confidence, momentum, small wins, and feedback loops is critical to changing this mindset. Focusing on key activities is the simplest way to instill discipline, to build confidence, and to establish expectations that can grow with the individual over time.

Designing your plans and initiatives to highlight small wins fuels momentum, reinforces skill development, and creates an environment of success and winning. This approach requires vision, patience, and discipline to change the sustained trajectory of your individuals and teams over time.

One of the keys to the Move the Middle approach is the power of small wins and the aggregation of marginal improvement and gains. All outcomes are a direct result of activities, behaviors and habits - habits being the most powerful and predictable in driving long term change in personal lives and corporate success.

If you always rely on home runs to win games or make your numbers, you've missed a key part of sport and business, which is the fact that singles, doubles, and great execution day in and day out wins championships.

What are small wins and how do they differ from participation awards earned by kids for showing up to play soccer, baseball, and every other sport?

Small wins are demonstrations of progress and achievements. With a clear understanding of all the key metrics, you can determine their correlation and relationship to progress and winning. I refer to these as trigger wins because each successive win triggers greater confidence, effort, and the next possible win.

Small wins are in everything you do and experience. The world of endurance sports is perfect for illustrating the principle. The first triathlon was held in 1974 by a group of athletes in San Diego.

After a series of small successes, the Ironman was conceived and hosted by a handful of athletes four years later. In those early days, people signed up, showed up, and did it. The rest of the world looked at them and thought them odd.

Forty years later, competitors who aren't even athletic sign up for Ironman triathlons and complete the race in the designated time. Go to an Ironman race finish after 10:00 pm and watch for the last two hours of the race as hundreds of athletes come streaming through the finish lines smiling, crawling, puking. Each cries with joy, overwhelmed that they accomplished something so inconceivable that it leaves them in awe.

Small wins create a domino effect. When you knock one down, it can knock down a domino many times its size. Think of the power of that principle consistently applied to your business.

Are you waiting until the end of the year to give your employees a review and hand out a big bonus, or have you created an environment where you recognize small wins? Are your managers celebrating those wins or are they going unnoticed and unrecognized?

Celebrating big wins and achievements is natural in life, but the leaders and managers who leverage the consistency and momentum of small wins have a better chance of sustaining performance.

Ask yourself as a manager and leader, can you point to your small wins and measure their effect?

The Middle Challenge...

✓ The key to testing the power of small wins on your team is to focus on activities, which are the easiest way to establish expectations, instill discipline, and build experience and confidence.

✓ Track progress as it fuels momentum, demonstrates skills and growth, and signals that change is possible.

✓ Determine up front how you're going to recognize progress. Take the time to publicly recognize those individuals or teams that have a new PR or make progress.

✓ We found that small wins triggered bigger wins so carefully maintain a balance between effort, results, and recognition.

Photo of Jack and "Coach" Gerry Halphen at mile 11 during Jack's first Ironman race in Panama City, Florida.

 Bottom Line: One of the keys to the move the middle approach is the power of small wins and the aggregation of marginal improvement and gains.

Oprah and the Middle

One of my all-time favorite stories of a middle performer is Oprah Winfrey. Those who have heard her story know she wasn't always on top. As a matter of fact, she started like all top performers: at the bottom.

Aside from having an incredible mind and being blessed with a beautiful spirit and generous heart, Oprah didn't see herself as a middle performer. In fact, Oprah was fired from her first job as a newscaster because she injected too much emotion into her stories. It was that same emotion that made her the wealthiest female in entertainment and one of the wealthiest people on the planet. If you took away her wealth and popularity, I bet she would admit she struggles with the same challenges most Americans do, like weight and fitness.

If Oprah was just another middle-aged female working in your office without all the money and fame, how would you treat her? As her manager, would you have any idea what she was capable of producing for your company?

How many Oprahs do you have working at your company today? Are they members of a team or do they feel the isolation that comes from being ignored or mismanaged? And if you knew they were there, how differently would you treat them? What would you do to encourage and nurture their potential?

In the world of entertainment Oprah is a top performer, but in other areas of her life Oprah is just like you and me. Oprah as a runner is a Middle Performer!

Do you think could you run a 4:29:15 marathon at a 10:16 per mile pace? Guess what? That was Oprah's race time for the marathon - which is the average of the "middle" for marathon times in 2014. The average finishing time for men in U.S. marathons was 4:19:27, and the average finishing time for women was 4:44:19.

She doesn't look like the middle because of what she accomplished in other areas of her life, but as a runner she's a middle performer! In all honesty the comparison is flawed and misleading; Oprah wasn't average, she was fifteen minutes FASTER than the average marathon time for women.

If you compared Oprah to her age group, she SMOKED the average. If you compared her time to the average of all marathons run in Ironman races she would be up there with the top performers in her gender and age group. Now let's take her 10:16 per mile average and compare it to half marathon splits. She wasn't a middle performer in my book. She was a ROCK STAR!

Without her fame the normal manager sees an overweight, middle-aged female and thinks, "average." But when Oprah gets up in the morning, she doesn't aspire to average and neither do your employees.

<u>One personal observation I want you to consider is that the key to Oprah's success is she didn't hire a manager to help her reach her goals. She hired a coach!</u> The manager would have sat at his or her desk and held meetings to update his boss on Oprah's performance. If she fell below a certain performance level I'm sure she would have been put on a performance plan or fired.

If we mapped Oprah's running path to stardom, where do you think she went from average to good and good to Rock Star? What small wins created that trigger event to give her the courage to go beyond her dreams and aspirations?

How did her beliefs drive her feelings, activities, and behaviors? What were the results that built the necessary momentum to change her opinion of her athletic self and everyone around her? What if she took a different career path without the opportunity to succeed and grow, do you think she would still have that long list of accomplishments?

Think about why so many individuals with potential wash out and quit when they are far ahead of their peers? My experience and belief say it's because <u>success is a progressive process and not a singular event.</u>

I have always believed that the biggest challenge is getting leaders and managers to listen to their people rather than doing all the talking. Quit managing and start coaching! If you're talking all the time, how can you ever figure out where your talent is headed and how you might be able to help them optimize their chance of getting there? Moreover, how can you learn from others' experiences? There is a reason the good Lord gave us two ears and one mouth.

If you're struggling with a complacent middle that you don't think is making the most of their opportunities, you might want to start with the individual that can do the most to change the outcome: you!

Middle Challenge questions...

✓ If asked, would your employees say they view their boss as a manager or coach?

✓ Does your leadership training reinforce the tactics of a manager or the role of a coach?

✓ Are there people in the middle who, if properly inspired and coached, could become top performers?

Bottom Line: One of the great lessons I learned from all of our employee initiatives was the power of the manager to change outcomes. The best managers were the ones that made the critical connection between goals, motivation, and results. Get the managers to think like coaches and watch the middle come to play at a different level of intensity.

The Middle Mindset

Ever hear the saying that "the most successful businessmen were C students?" President Harry S Truman was even quoted saying "C students run the world." It's not always the case but it highlights an important aspect of life, business, and success. GPAs aren't always the best indicators of success because grades don't necessarily reflect effort, ability, interest, skills, or potential. When college students graduate, they begin a very different part of life's journey that many times rewards effort, risk-taking, and perseverance over talent and intelligence.

The difference between success and failure has more to do with your progress and position than your actual performance. Simply put, it's the effect of the Rubber Band or Dynamic Tension that controls your experience.

Going back to the analogy of the C student, the reason the student gets Cs but is capable of As and Bs is because there's no Dynamic Tension engaging them, good or bad. In my experience positive Dynamic Tension creates positive effects while negative Dynamic Tension creates toxic environments. Throughout the book my intent is to show managers, leaders, and parents how the principles of positively applied Dynamic Tension can inspire, motivate, and transform individuals and teams.

The Rubber Band is such a powerful analogy for the principles of Moving the Middle because so many of the dynamics of engaging individuals and teams require a certain degree of stretching and tension to bring out their best. Let me explain. When business is "good" the tension on performance is loosened, but when businesses are in a crisis mode the Dynamic Tension rises and people come to work with a different level of commitment and intensity.

More times than not it's your Middle Performers that rise to the challenge and create the most impact on performance. You might ask where were those Middle Performers before the crisis, but I would ask you how were you using the Rubber Band prior to the crisis to create the right amount of Dynamic Tension.

Below are the beliefs, activities, and behaviors that generally define the different performance groups. Since performance is just a snapshot in time and a reflection of the Dynamic Tension in play, use these definitions to better understand where your people fall on the spectrum and what activities might be fueling this belief. Remember that 80% are not in the Top, so everything you do should be to get and keep the 80% not performing to their potential to become more like the Top performers.

Top 20%

They set goals to achieve and 'be the best.' Competitive, driven by status motivation. They want to know where they stand in relation to the goal and compared to others (progress feedback). Love the game, being the best, the competition, and the social recognition that comes with being the best.

High discretionary effort, achievement-oriented, thriving on recognition, enthusiastic, optimistic, looking for ways to improve, enjoy work, and are emotionally connected to results. Demonstrate what performance is possible, strong work ethic, highly engaged.

They stay late and come in early. They outwork, out-prepare, and in time their skills become better as a result.

Middle 60%

Comfortable being in the middle, perform below their real potential, not driven by money, respond when challenged, but backslide to 'cruise' when pressure is off, recognition is more valuable than cash incentives, rarely recognized because their performance tends to be in average range, moderately engaged.

Good as measured by average, but not great. If they were motivated like top performers, they could and do at times deliver performance on that level. They demonstrate the skills, experience, and ability to deliver results, but rarely over-achieve or live up to their potential.

Bottom 20%

Perform below expectations and view work as a job, not a place to succeed or thrive; low energy, lack commitment, not emotionally connected, demonstrate little to no discretionary effort.

When they work hard, they can be a catalyst on the team and inspire the team even though they may never be better than average.

If not properly handled these employees can erode the sense of team, undermine leadership, and pollute the environment.

So how do we disrupt this thinking and feeling of complacency? Successful leaders change the rules of the game by changing the perception of what matters and inspiring their teams to work together towards a common goal.

If you want to see this theory play out, go to a high school cross country meet and watch the kids finish the last half mile of a 5k race. The race is usually won by the kid that runs in second or third place throughout the race. The strength of the runner lies in their perception of their position rather than who is the stronger runner.

In cross country, there's a lot of equally important races going on within the race. The first 5–6 runners across the finish line contribute to the overall score. The team with the lowest score factored by each respective runner's finish time wins.

Kids find their equals as the race unfolds and as the race nears the finish runners are now competing for as high of a finish as possible to help the team win. Who are the kids behind the leaders competing against? The leaders or the kids in close proximity to them? Bingo! People compare themselves to their peer groups.

One of our strongest influences is driven by those individuals in the closest proximity to our ability and performance. Understanding how this affects the perceptions of the middle is a critical step in the process.

The problem if you compare an employee's performance to anyone outside their reference group is that that's not who they identify with. Case in point: if you constantly compare a middle performer to a top performer what they're quietly saying to themselves is that the comparison is meaningless to them for more reasons than you can imagine.

Only when there's a perceived opportunity or advantage do we see employees and athletes compete all the way to the finish. More often than not they give up early in the process although they'd never admit it.

Let those words sink in a few minutes. If you're comparing your middle performers to your top performers you're creating a toxic environment for everyone on the team. As my friend always reminds me, "comparison is the thief of joy," but I would add it impacts motivation, desire, and perseverance even more.

Welcome to the mindset of the middle performer. The mindset of the top and bottom performers is also a big, unseen obstacle to change.

In the world of business, the same holds true when operating contests or incentives designed to improve performance. Based on the program's design we found we could accurately predict who would win, how long individuals would perform before dropping off or quitting, and how performance overall would impact results. Our phrase for these predictions was "likelihood to sustain."

In one case, our client was in the process of launching a new security product to select markets. At first glance, everything looked positive with new customers being acquired and overall revenue growing at an impressive rate.

When we took a closer look at the performance data, we realized that the growth was being driven by expansion to new markets and not increases in sales from their existing stores.

As we studied the data we realized that the stores and individuals that had experienced early success and reached a certain level of new sales per rep were the ones growing, while the majority of the stores had low adoption rates and never reached the tipping point of success. The adoption rates of their middle performers predicted success better than any other measure of performance.

When we shared the data with the client, his team explained that they were already aware of the situation and were getting ready to remedy the problem with a bigger customer discount and bigger incentives for the sales reps. Guess how the story ends? The product continued to slide and spent the next few years on the verge of extinction. The problem wasn't with the product— I bought it and it was very good. The problem was in the mindset of the middle.

The data clearly demonstrated that once a rep had four sales per month they were "likely to sustain" performance or grow but if they never reached that level of performance or fell below three sales per month they would lose interest, expertise, familiarity with the product, and performance would follow. Five months after the launch, the reps became so out of touch with the technical aspects of the product that the managers typically had to complete the sale because their reps didn't know how.

As we peeled back the onion on the product launch to the reps we noticed a number of flaws in the strategy. Marketing clearly thought this would be a customer-driven product. Training clearly thought the reps didn't need to know how the product worked or was different because it was so good it would sell itself. The compensation team clearly thought this was an easy sale and only rewarded the top sellers in their incentive design.

The middle performers continued to compare themselves to their peers, creating a self-fulfilling prophecy that not only minimized the success of the product launch but in time destroyed the product as a viable service to their customers. Since the product designs only highlighted and rewarded the top performers, the middle quietly cruised well below their potential, undermining the success of the product for the company.

Think about it. <u>Every time the Middle spoke with their customers, their lack of confidence, motivation, and skills undermined every interaction. Instead of everyone becoming promoters, the employees became detractors.</u>

This isn't an uncommon performance issue. In fact, it's at the heart of all companies launching new products and piloting new ideas. <u>The beliefs of the team become the beliefs of the customers, which places an even greater emphasis on your focus on the middle and not just your top performers.</u>

As a leader of a large national team I saw this first hand as we launched a culture change initiative within our Client Services division. The shift in behaviors, activities, and performance were easily measured and highly visible. The teams with strong middles became the early adopters while the teams with weak middles required multiple efforts to reach an acceptable level of understanding and skill.

Our key takeaway was that the top performers that were the most demanding of our resources had the least amount of influence on the team and our success. The better predictor of success was the influence and mindset of the middle performers.

Middle Challenge questions...

✓ What are the mindsets of your middle and top performers?

✓ Are those mindsets positively or negatively affecting performance?

✓ Who are each of your teams' greatest influencers?

✓ Are they a positive or negative influence on behavior and performance?

✓ Are your programs designed to engage the middle or top performers?

✓ How can you use this knowledge to change the dynamics of the group and to reinforce the positive influencers?

Bottom Line: Our greatest influence is driven by those individuals in the closest proximity to our ability and performance. Understanding how this affects the mindset of the middle is the first critical step in the process.

CHAPTER 2

THE MANAGER AND THE TEAM

"Management is not a function of playing head scorekeeper, where all you have to do is hang medals on the winners. Management is a function you perform to influence the outcome of the race. Management is recognizing those runners during the race who have never won but have run the 1st 100 yards faster than they did before."

– Ferdinand F. Fournies,
Coaching for Improved Work Performances

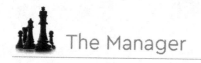

Your Greatest Obstacle to Success is You

Simply put, you are the problem and you are the solution. We are all a product of our environment, education, experiences, aspirations, desires and habits. There are a lot of elements that go into that statement but in the end, it's all there. <u>To change our results, we have to believe that doing something different will lead to a different outcome.</u>

If you want to get the most from your team, it starts with your beliefs. What are your beliefs that bias the way you view and treat middle performers? If you have a team of less than 10, I'd write down each of their names and then note why you think they are stuck in the middle. Here are some thought starters:

- No effort.

- Don't care.

- Stopped trying.

- Don't have the skills.

- Too established or too new.

- Not engaged. Wrong job.

- Not qualified.

- In over their heads.

- Not organized.

If you're not honest with this simple exercise your biases will undermine every attempt you make to engage this critical group of people. Go ahead and write down those beliefs about your people and performance and we can check back later so you can assess where you started and how far you go in your own development.

Here's where it becomes interesting. Now, on that same list write down who is responsible for getting your team inspired, skilled and motivated.

Last column: (and this is where I want you to be brutally honest with your assessment) why do your team members feel that way?

In most organizations from business to sports and even education, it's the blame game. It's the student's fault that they're not learning. It's the child's fault that they don't care. It's the athletes fault that they don't have the necessary skills to keep up with their competition. And it's the employee's fault that they no longer perform up to expectations or their ability.

The teacher, parent, coach, and manager are not put in these roles to be passive guides on the road of life but are expected to be instrumental leaders in helping their students, kids, athletes, and workers realize their gifts and achieve their potential.

When you signed up for the job of manager, what did you sign up for? To make your targets despite your team or to lead and motivate your team to improve their performance and beat their team best?

How you treat people determines how they will respond. It sounds simple but my bet is that most middle performers are delivering average results because of the way they feel towards their manager more than any other reason. The data on why people quit their jobs says essentially the same thing.

The

number one

reason people

quit their jobs is

because of their

relationship with

their **boss**.

Long before the employee engagement surveys were the big trend in corporate America we could walk into a call center or technician work center and tell instantly based on the team chemistry how well the manager was performing. No need to go through a long survey to see what was clearly happening in real time in that work center.

But when you would discuss the performance of the team with the same manager he would tell you all the issues he was experiencing with his people. How you treat your people is determining how well they perform every day.

I had just finished writing this chapter and wanted to see how it would apply to something as simple as athletes running in a race. I was planning to cheer on friends doing a half-Ironman in Chattanooga and figured with over 2,000 athletes in attendance I could conduct a fairly large-scale experiment without much effort. The experiments were centered on how the athletes would respond based on different stimuli.

The plan was to provide feedback to the athletes similar to what an employee might experience at work.

1. The first interaction would provide a neutral emotional interaction.

2. The second interaction was a quick personal interaction with each of them and promoting the aid station ahead with food, ice and drinks.

3. The third interaction was designed around celebrating their efforts, progress and accomplishments.

What I wanted to see was how my interaction with the athletes changed their response and experience in the moment.

The half-Ironman in Chattanooga requires the athletes to swim 1.2 miles, bike 56 miles, and run 13.1 miles. Fast athletes like the pros and age group winners can finish the race in just over four hours while slower athletes finish closer to 7–8 hours.

During the first interaction, I stood alongside the run course (the athletes had already swum 1.2 miles and biked 56 miles by the time we started the experiment) and clapped and said "nice job" and "way to go." I purposely didn't look them in the eyes or call out their names even though their names are printed in large letters on their race bibs for this very purpose. The athletes passed by me, heads down without much of a flicker of excitement and acknowledgement. I get it... they were tired.

The second interaction was an hour later. For this part of the experiment I planted myself at the base of a pretty difficult hill. At the top of the hill was an aid station, with water, food and ice. This time I called them by name, clapped and encouraged them to stay strong because at the top of that hill were refreshments, ice water and a nice downhill as a reward. Same people different response. They were running up the hardest hill on the course and laughing and thanking me! <u>By the way the fast guys were already finished with the race... these were the middle performers and with just a little bit of encouragement they came to life on the hardest part of the course. The more I cheered the happier they got, the stronger they felt the better they performed.</u>

The last experiment was an hour later and designed to throw an all-out celebration to see how the athletes would respond. This time I positioned myself at the bottom of a long bridge with plenty of time to get eye contact with the athletes. The big difference was this was now late in the race. The athletes had their heads down and were quietly shuffling along and completely drained. Most of the athletes had been racing for well over 5–6 hours with the finish line a good hour away. This is a dark time in a race because athletes are tired and depleted and still have to run six more miles which now seems like an eternity.

This was clearly my favorite experience and most appreciated by the athletes. This time I called them by name and celebrated what they accomplished by telling them how strong they looked, how amazing they were, said how proud they should be of themselves. You could literally see the athletes' enthusiasm rise, their pace quicken and the smiles get bigger than a 5-year-old at their birthday!

A few weeks later I met up with one of the athletes and she gave me a big hug. I asked what the hug was all about and she explained that a few minutes prior to seeing me that she had decided to quit the race. She still had another six-mile loop before the finish and was exhausted. She said when she saw me and I told her she was looking so good and how proud she should be of her effort it flipped a switch and she went on to finish the race... her first ever half-Ironman. She also finished on the podium and was recognized as one of the tops in her age group.

Think of the implications of this experiment in your company. If you want to change the outcome or your people you first have to change how you treat them and their experience. What you think, say and do is either holding your team back or helping you win. If you're having to fire good people, it's probably you and not them.

One of the biggest revelations that most managers and leaders have as I talk about changing performance is that how we treat and view people is how they perform. If you tell your son/daughter they're stupid or uncoordinated they'll respond the same way that your employees do when you tell them they are average.

Yes, at first we are going to talk up our people and in time that talk will result in better action and positive results. Nothing will ever change until we change those long-held beliefs that have been holding us back.

Middle Challenge questions...

✓ What are your personal biases about the top, middle and low performers? About their drive, skills, attitude, experience, knowledge, commitment, and contribution?

✓ Where did you get those beliefs?

✓ Do you treat different performance groups differently?

✓ If so, how and why?

✓ Who do you spend your time with at work? Low, middle, top?

✓ What kind of impact are you getting from your time and effort?

✓ How would your people say you add value to their performance?

Bottom Line: Always begin with positive intent and know the accountability of the team is the responsibility of the manager and is reflected in his/her team performance.

Play like a Champion

Lou Holtz (former head coach of Notre Dame football) put up the sign "Play Like a Champion Today" outside the locker room en-route to the field. He wanted his players to hit the sign as they headed for practice or for a game. It was that positive imprinting, seeding and reinforcing of the values they aspired to as a player and team that he wanted them to see and recommit to every day when it mattered most.

Holtz knew that how a player thought or perceived affected how the player felt, and how they felt dictated how they played and thus their results. Inspirational and aspirational slogans may sound trite but if you want to change performance it comes from changing the way individuals think and feel.

James Allen wrote "Man's mind may be likened to a garden, which may be intelligently cultivated or allowed to run wild; but whether cultivated or neglected, it must and will, bring forth." Although these words were written over a 100 years ago they are just as applicable today.

What thoughts and images are you putting in the minds of your people as the gardener of your team? Good seed or are you allowing it to run wild with weeds and bad seed?

There is no science to this; it's all head and heart. Holtz wasn't assured that "Play Like a Champion Today" would trigger a response so he tried and now decades later it stands as one of the most recognized motivational phrases in sports.

Holtz wasn't only good at developing motivating phrases, when he took over the head coaching job at Notre Dame the performance of the team had been struggling for years with 5 wins and 6 losses in its previous season. Holtz turned around the program and went on to lead the team to an undefeated season in 1988 and the national championship. He had an overall record of 100 wins, 32 losses and 2 ties at Notre Dame.

The best coaches put the player at the center of the experience just like companies need to put the manager and employee at the center of their experience. What do you want your team to think, say and do as a result of the experience?

This proposal is a dramatic shift from the normal process of "what do we want our managers and employees to do and how can we get them to do it?" If you start with the employee you humanize your approach. What are they thinking and feeling? Do they have the skills? Why is it that whatever we want done is not getting accomplished? How have they responded to previous initiatives? Ultimately how is what they're feeling translating to how they're performing and can we change that with our approach?

When I think back over all the employee performance initiatives we developed and launched, it was clear when we hit homeruns and when we hit foul balls. If we had a hard time gaining consensus it was a sign we weren't in tune with what was happening in the field. Holtz was so in tune with what was important to his players that he could put a phrase on a sign and the world would understand it without any explanation.

What Holtz didn't say on that sign was almost as masterful as what he chose to put on it. Why don't you think he said anything about the importance of his top performers, or what would happen if you're on the bottom? And why do you think he never mentioned the players in the middle? Holtz knew that leading a team was all about leading with a positive vision and voice and that making his players feel they were part of something special and a winning team was the most important thing to get everyone to give their best effort.

Our best themes were never as good as *Play Like A Champion Today* but one of our design meetings resulted in one of the best themes we ever created. The theme was so quickly adopted by every manager and leader in the organization that it was alive before anyone ever saw it in print.

The way it came about was the team was planning for the next year and reviewing the conversations we were having with the field. We invited a number of managers from the field to join the session. In the group was one young manager who changed everything that day.

Our intent was to test some concepts and validate some possible themes with the managers and get their feedback. The managers quietly listened to our ideas and then a young manager from Birmingham Alabama stood up and took off his shirt. Under that shirt was a T-shirt that had the words "I AM FIVE STAR."

The manager clearly understood his role as a gardener, had been planting good seeds in the minds of his team and as a result...they brought forth and were one of the top teams in the company. He elevated the status and importance of the initiative and reinforced it with his team in everything he did. I AM FIVE STAR was such a powerful statement that it transcended every communication, training, recognition and celebration that we delivered for the next few years. One of the Senior Vice Presidents was such a fan of the idea that he had a shirt made up for himself and wore it to his company town hall meeting.

The key about seeding, gardening and getting people to play like a champion is all about creating and fostering a positive environment that encourages employees to want to work and win...together.

These principles in sports seem so obvious because we naturally expect players on a team to play together and to complement each other's strengths. We expect the teams to work together to out-work, out-hustle and out-play their opponents. We expect the coach to lead with a positive vision and plan rather than demoralizing and ignoring those players struggling to make it.

Why do we expect to see it in sports but don't see that same leadership and expect that same chemistry in the work place? If we walked your offices, stores or warehouses would we feel that aspirational sense of *Play Like A Champion*? Who owns it? You do, don't you? Even if you're a first level manager in a company of thousands of employees you can change the future of your company by inspiring your team and watching that energy go viral.

Middle Challenge questions...

✓ What are the seeds you've been planting?

✓ How have they affected your team's performance?

✓ If asked, what would your peers and employees say about your approach?

✓ Are there some obvious changes you need to make as a coach in terms of leading with a positive vision?

✓ What's your "Play Like A Champion Today" mantra?

 Bottom Line: It starts with you. The coach puts the player at the center of the experience just like companies need to put the manager and employees at the center of their experience. What do you want them to think, say and do as a result of the experience?

Finding Strength in the Middle

One of my favorite "Dad experiences" was coaching my son Max in 7th and 8th grade basketball.

I wasn't a great player growing up but before I started caddying I played all the time. My brothers were older and much better players, which made me work twice as hard when I got a chance to play with them. I may have been tall but they valued skills, intensity and drive over height in the style of ball they played.

During those summers, we played from the minute the sun came up until it got dark. My mom didn't have to go looking for her kids...we lived for basketball and were always out behind the house shooting hoops.

When I saw the opportunity to coach Max, I was all over it.

Coaches in this league drafted their teams like the pros and probably had more at stake when it came to their social status with the other families. I really didn't know all the kids, so my older son Morgan went with me to the draft to help me select the kids.

It was obvious that the bigger kids at this age had an advantage. Seeing the other coaches immediately go for the biggest kids, I asked Morgan to help pick out smaller, faster kids who would work hard and have a good attitude.

My first pick was my son Max, not because he was my son but because I loved his passion for the sport!

Over the next several rounds, as the big kids were selected, we went small and fast with Morgan's recommendations.

By the time the draft ended, from the looks from the other dads it was obvious that I drafted the worst team ever and they had at least one easy win ahead in the season.

That's not what happened.

Our team played every practice and game with the understanding that we had the advantage. We were going to outrun every man on the court. When the ball hit the ground, the kids dove after it. Our defense swarmed whoever had the ball and pressed at every chance.

If you put these kids on another team, they would be middle-to-low performers. But on our team, they became an undefeated high performing team that won the championship.

After the season, I got one of the nicest compliments from a parent of one of my favorite players. We did such a good job coaching and encouraging their son that he really thought he was great player. I responded back that he was, because he was a team player.

When joined with a purpose, teams with strong middles beat teams with more talent every day.

David Scobey, the president of the client I worked with, often said that "the best managers don't make their numbers based on a few top performers, but make sure that everyone on their team makes their numbers."

I wrote that in my playbook twelve years ago and still refer back to it when discussing the difference between average and great managers.

The best managers have the best middles.

I suggest you look at the manager data to find these insights, correlations and relationship with the middle performers. What does your bias and experience tell you it is? We find that great managers have better performing teams, less variability in performance and more individuals on their team achieving their goals than average managers do.

The reason this so critical to your success is that it's less expensive and more inspiring to engage teams than to spend all your time and money recruiting "better" performers. People respond to managers and coaches that create a culture of winning and recognition.

Everyone is inspired and motivated by different things. Understanding their team's individual and collective motivation and tapping into those elements is what the great manager does.

Having worked with thousands of managers in these programs we heard the stories and realized how different employees reacted to different encouragement and recognition.

One size does not fit all and it's the job of the manager to know the difference. Take the case of a manger with a team of 15 technicians. Everyone was at different stages of life, tenure and experience and has different motives. The technician with four kids had a different set of values and needs than the young single guy starting out in his career.

The technician with four kids admits that more money would be nice to help pay bills. But what really motivates him is the recognition of going the extra mile and ability to earn points and take his family on vacations and buy them Christmas gifts.

When the manager understands this key element, he works with the technician to make sure that he made a point to show appreciation for staying late at the customer's office to fix their service. He also made a point to ask about what trip or gifts he was saving up towards and how close he was to his goal. <u>Making it about the technician rather than the manager transformed their relationship and took a middle performer to a consistent top performer.</u>

The same manager learned his new technician starting his career wasn't driven by those same motivations. He spent time getting to know the technician and learned that he was motivated by learning new things and had a goal of earning a new flat screen TV, couch and bed for his new and empty apartment.

In each situation, the manager and the technicians worked together to find specific ways they could improve performance, which was a far easier coaching session than simply telling them if the numbers weren't there, they'd lose their jobs.

Fear and the stick can be effective short-term motivators. If you want to achieve sustainable results in the long run, the motivation should stress positive behaviors and outcomes.

The great managers lead people who deliver the results while average managers lean on the numbers and targets.

Middle Challenge questions...

✓ It all starts with you. Ask your team what their motivations are. Get below the surface answers until you hear answers that address family, career, and what's important to them.

✓ Listen. Employee satisfaction and engagement surveys are worthless. Go talk to your people. Word will get out if you're sincere in your desire to help.

✓ Take notes and show you care by making changes that address their goals and values.

✓ Share the feedback every time you meet with your team and employees. It shows you're listening and care about what was said.

✓ Do something small and build momentum.

Bottom Line: When joined with a purpose, teams with strong middles beat teams with more talent every day.

Do Managers Matter?

I was running down the D-Concourse at Atlanta's Hartsfield Jackson International Airport and was close to missing my flight due to the abnormally long security lines. It was post 9/11 and missing flights and getting booked on another flight was brutal because the airlines were overbooking all the flights, and everyone was in the same bag.

If you didn't arrive at security a good two hours before your flight your mind was already playing the "what if" scenario on possible flight options to your next destination.

In the middle of the chaos of standing in the security line and running for the flight I kept seeing a New Yorker magazine cover with the title "do parents really matter?" When I got to the gate, the flight was delayed an hour because of bad weather and despite dripping with sweat and being completely out of breath, I was thrilled.

The title of the magazine had me intrigued and with my extra airport time, I stopped into the news shop across from the gate. I began to read the article and discovered a principle so profound that it would change my life as a parent and leader.

In a nutshell, a grandmother came up with a theory that when a child is born, the influence of the parents is 100%. As the child gets older that influence diminishes so that by the time they become teenagers their peers are stronger influencers and when they get to college as a parent you have practically no influence at all.

At the time, we had three young children at home. As I read the article and thought of its implications on our family it was clear we needed to focus more energy while we still could influence the outcome of their lives.

The article was scary because it showed that my older kids were on the verge of being influenced as much by their friends as by their parents. It was my first wake-up call as a parent that the clock was ticking and based on my travel schedule I was losing the opportunity to influence the very essence of what was most important to me... my family.

While working on a client initiative years later, a question came up from the client asking, "do managers really matter?" I quickly got up and drew the graph from the magazine article and told the story of my experience as a parent.

The team started diving into the data on tenure and performance and realized that what they described for a child was the same for an employee. Early on the manager was the biggest influence on the individual's growth, beliefs and development (good and bad) but as they met colleagues and made friends those individuals had a greater influence on their attitude, skills, experience, aspirations, and engagement.

The more we looked the more we realized that yes, the manager was important early on but if the team didn't trust, like, or respect the manager it became evident in their engagement and performance.

What we came to better understand is that great managers do not interact with new team members in the same way as their tenured staff. When employees are new they have a thousand questions.

If the manager doesn't guide that effort early on, progress is delayed and expectations on both sides of the aisle aren't met. As the employee gets further into their position and sees their peers thriving while they're struggling it definitely impacts their belief and confidence.

If you've ever dealt with a teenager that's struggling with school, parents, or social life you understand the power and influence of their peer group. The same is true as this individual looks around and doesn't get the necessary coaching from their manager.

As team members display the necessary skills, knowledge, and experience to earn more autonomy in their role, if the manager is still micro-managing that individual it results in massive frustration. Teaching managers how to identify where their team members are progressing and how to interact with them is almost as important in their success as a manager as it is as a parent.

Helicopter parents of teenagers get the same response at home as micro managers get in the work place and the outcome is just as costly. Stress and anxiety don't help the situation; rather it creates a toxic environment and resentment from the employees and team.

Do managers matter? Yes, but if their style is not cognizant of the needs of the individuals on the team it can not only frustrate everyone, but it can sabotage the very thing the manager is trying to build. Those frustrations are at the root of the top reasons employees quit their jobs.

What would your team say about you? If it's a one size fits all approach to the team that may sound like a compliment but if they're not talking about honesty, mutual trust and fairness than you might have problems.

An easy way to build your personal plan moving forward is to map or graph each of your team members and assess their skills, knowledge and experience. Holtz knew that how a player thought or perceived affected how the player felt, and how they felt dictated how they played and thus their results.

The Middle Challenge...

✓ If you have team members that demonstrate strong skills, knowledge, and experience, let them lead.

- It could be that they mentor team members or work on project teams that acknowledge their ability and allow them the opportunity to contribute at another level.

- Who better than these natural leaders on your team to raise the bar and create a positive social influence on the team.

✓ If you have team members somewhere in the middle on performance but strong in the areas of skills, knowledge and experience give them a chance to work on projects and with teams that could benefit from their expertise.

- The increased responsibility and recognition tends to have a positive effect on meaning and motivation resulting in improved performance.

✓ Team members needing more knowledge, skills and experience that are partnered with their peers will benefit from the increased interaction and this allows them to build deeper relationships on the team.

<u>Bottom Line:</u> Early on the manager is the biggest influence on the individual employee's growth, beliefs, and development (good and bad) but as they meet colleagues and make friends those individuals have a greater influence on their attitude, skills, experience, aspirations, and engagement. Know where each of your team members are on the spectrum and adjust your style to complement their needs and opportunities for growth and development.

Winning with Skills over Technology

Let's address the elusive and false gods of new technology. I know many of the generation that is reading this have been raised by watching DVDs, listening to CDs and iPods, and believe the need for college has all but been eliminated by the speed and accuracy of Google and hold on to the belief that the next generation of the iPhone will solve all of our problems. For all the promises of technology, corporate America still struggles with an ever-increasing disengaged and unmotivated middle.

What happens between the concept, implementation and adoption of all these changes to improve performance? Why, despite the many investments in technology, does the middle stay in the middle? Why do the same issues that existed in human performance 30 years ago remain unchanged today?

Could the answer be that leaders and managers today are more focused on the promise of technology rather than the adoption of new skills and value of personal improvement and performance? Does your company spend more money rolling out a new CRM system than they spend on the training and development of their people?

Where you spend your money is a neon sign for your values and priorities as a company. When training and development initiatives are cut in favor of the newest technology you are clearly communicating that importance and relevance to your people.

Of course, you're screaming as you think of all the improvements that have been made from a technology point of view to deliver fewer errors, improve compliance, expand reporting, and give leadership better visibility in all the key metrics.

Technology has advanced our ability to communicate, improve controls, and eliminated countless jobs but for all it's done, it rarely if ever improves the discretionary effort of your employees. If it did you wouldn't be reading this book.

Skill development is one of the least understood motivations of your workforce. Giving your team opportunities to enhance or refine their skills can be one of the most powerful forces of personal motivation.

The great companies and cultures understand this and invest as much in the development of their people as they do in other areas of their businesses because they know the power of an engaged employee.

Giving employees status motivation that comes from advancement creates social currency on the team and in their personal lives. When employees become specialists, experts or mentors because of their skill levels it signals to the world that they are being recognized for their leadership and contributions.

The way they feel and perform is a result of how they're being treated. But the opposite is also true so when companies cut training to fund technology they communicate a very different message that undermines the attitudes and discretionary effort of the life blood of the companies: the middle 60%. It's why the middle becomes complacent.

You are not alone; it's the same in almost every corner of the world. A good example of this cultural shift is in golf. For all the technology advances in golf the average handicap and score is the same as it was when I caddied 40 years ago.

Golfers have better drivers, irons, putters, balls, and even devices that link with satellites to give you yardages to the hole but for all those advancements the average handicap and scores of the middle haven't advanced one shot.

The technology is better, no question about it. The balls fly farther, the design of the clubs makes it easier to hit a better shot and everything about the sport on the technology front has improved but the most important element in the game, the player, hasn't improved.

Golf is a skill sport. The player with the best skills and not the best technology wins more often than not. The more golfers rely on technology and less on skill development for improvement the more their game deteriorates.

Despite more investment in better technology without an equal or greater amount of practice scores get worse not better. Skills and better scores are earned with effort and not in the pro shop buying better technology.

The same is true of cycling. The weight of bikes has gone down so much with the improvement of technology that the weight of the bikes used in professional races are not allowed to go below a certain weight minimum. The bike times for races on the same courses in the same conditions using the newest and improved technology deliver only small improvements with the best riders.

When the newest technology comes available to the average riders it always demands a premium price, but the middle riders rarely move forward and the gap between the middle and the top riders rarely narrows.

If you're going to bank on technology like new CRM systems to save your company or improve your growth you have to go beyond the technology to your employees' behavior to realize the improvement. The key to your success is the adoption of the new skills to leverage the technology in its optimal state.

Let's think about that new system that you've invested in deploying to your team. If you only get partial adoption of the technology, the system not only becomes a time suck for your people, but it'll feed you misleading data and insights in your business. The workarounds developed by your people might allow them to do their jobs, but the value of the tool will be seriously limited because of the quality of the data.

I recently met a very successful sales executive who took an early retirement from a large company. When asked why he left so much money on the table by retiring early he asked if I was familiar with the latest CRM company. I said I was and baited him with the comment "but didn't it make you more efficient and effective?" His answer was simple. "I not only lost a day a week in productivity by being anchored to the technology but I watched our company lose their focus on the customer only to be replaced by a focus on data."

This was a perfect case of a guy who was once a top performer that became disillusioned by leadership's love affair with technology and its promise for better reporting and increased accuracy in forecasting.

My experience with a similar reporting tool wasn't much better. For all the time, effort and resources applied to the technology my bet is a similar investment in their people and resources would have delivered a better result.

Middle Challenge questions...

Key questions to consider when evaluating the impact on technology on the middle:

✓ Whose (top, middle, bottom) performance will be impacted?

✓ What new skills or behavior are required to optimize the technology?

✓ What is the adoption rate in similar companies or industries?

✓ Who is really going to benefit from the new technology vs. who will be negatively be impacted by the new demands and requirements of the system?

✓ How is adoption measured and how does it impact performance?

Bottom Line: Technology has advanced our ability to communicate, improved controls, and eliminated countless jobs but for all it's done it rarely if ever improves the discretionary effort of your employees.

The Team

To Go Far, Go Together

Before you begin your design of the next great cultural change I encourage you to really understand your numbers. It's easy to throw out a cool campaign with a flashy new name and rich incentives but don't do it. It's not the answer for engaging your team and it's not going to drive sustained improvements.

In the movie *Moneyball*, the Oakland A's had about a third of the payroll budget that the most successful teams had. The coach and analyst, who become the stars of the show, quickly realized that they didn't have the budget to pay or play at the level of the competition. Their alternative approach was to recruit players leveraging the strength and talent of the middle performers to beat the best teams in the sport. The strategy worked as the A's took the world by storm and won the World Series.

The strategy defied all beliefs about staffing, recruiting and winning in America's favorite game. The approach no longer depended on signing a Top Player making more money than some of the top CEO's in the largest firms in America. The strategy relied on knowing the numbers and building a team that believed it could win and played together to leverage their strengths. There were no superstars; it was a team effort and highlighted the strength of a team energized by a common cause.

When word got out about the A's strategy, every baseball team in the league tried reshaping their teams around a stronger middle rather than over investing in top performers. The new strategy didn't last long because the top performer bias is so ingrained in managers' minds that many of the teams failed to adopt the real strategy behind Motivating the Middle.

Getting and keeping your middle performers emotionally engaged long enough to change their beliefs and sustain improved performance requires new thinking, strategies and understanding of what drives behavior.

Like the Oakland A's, triathlons and the Ironman have built their model on fueling the *Anything Is Possible* mantra of the Middle. At the athletic club I belonged to in Atlanta, we had around fifty middle-aged parents and professionals training on and off together for about five years. They were mostly moms and dads who got up early before work to get in a swim, spin, or run. When we started, the average workout length was 45–60 minutes and maybe a little longer on the weekends. Nothing out of the ordinary and probably what you're doing or capable of doing.

One year, three members of our group signed up for Ironman Florida. They were similar in talent and skill to the rest of the group but that year they changed the beliefs of everyone who watched them do progressively longer swims, bike rides, and runs. When they finished the race, something interesting happened: nine people from the group signed up the following year for the same race. A few years later 23 members of the group completed an Ironman together.

Ironman Couer D'Alene where 23 of our group completed the distance.

Of those 50 athletes, 30 went on to complete one or more Ironman races. Think about it. We didn't recruit top performers who wanted to do Ironman races. The athletes evolved from the beliefs, shared experiences, and social influences of the group.

How did so many athletes from one gym go from average to extraordinary? It was what happened within the group that changed the lives of everyone that joined us.

We experienced a similar outcome when we recognized that 2 vice president teams were on the verge of delivering a million dollars in referral revenue in the Just Ask customer referral program. We were wrapping up October numbers and noted that these 2 VPs could crest a million dollars if their referral volume didn't fall off its current trend.

The program owner started recognizing the efforts and promoting the possibility of these 2 VPs becoming the first and only members of the Million Dollar Club. What followed was like something out of the movies and as we soon found out the social influences of the teams were stronger than we understood.

The communications that had previously only been read by the senior managers were now being shared weekly with the front-line managers and their teams. The teams who both were both in Georgia started a little positive banter between each other challenging their teams to out-hustle and out-perform the other teams.

The numbers climbed and by December there was so much focus and energy on the race that the president of the division was throwing in double points for the winners and a cookout for the top team. The crazy thing was that every team in the company's revenue and activity went up as the energy from the race expanded. Positive energy and success were infectious and contagious.

That first year both VPs were honored by being inducted in the Million Dollar Club which we made up somewhere during the race. The people who made the greatest impact and difference in the outcome were the middle performers. It was amazing how it impacted their discretionary effort and performance.

The following year we went from 2 VPs to 9 in the Million Dollar Club. The next year we had 19 members in the Million Dollar Club and 2 members in the Two Million Dollar Club. All driven by the expectations and influence of the group.

You can't judge a person by what you see. It's what you don't see that matters. **The dynamics of a positive group environment trump any data, skill, or experience you believe to be an effective means of gauging talent, ability, and potential.**

Middle Challenge questions...

✓ Start by throwing out your top performers. Create an unbiased assessment of your team without the benefit of the top performers. Force yourself to honestly assess your talent and future potential across all the key criteria for success.

✓ Now look at your middle performers and go through a "what if" strategy session and consider what if the top performers all left tomorrow... how would you begin?

✓ Where are your strengths?

✓ What are those weaknesses that can easily be addressed? Start with the managers. The change begins with getting them to understand that they are here to coach up their players, lead a team and aren't there to manage people.

✓ Do you know the activities, behaviors, and experiences that are impacting your results? This is an imperative for you to develop and lead your managers because it's what they need to focus on to change performance.

 Bottom Line: Getting and keeping your middle performers emotionally engaged long enough to change their beliefs and sustain improved performance requires new thinking, strategies and understanding of what drives behavior. The dynamics of the group can trump the positional power of a manager every day.

Winning Together

The elasticity of a team's performance is controlled more by the perspective of the group than the expectations of the manager. Improvement and progress change these perspectives. <u>**Creating winning teams** rather than winning individuals is an important strategy because it transcends the rational motivation of the job by creating an emotional connection to the team.</u>

Throughout my experience the single biggest factor in winning was the manager and leader. I refer to this dynamic, countless times in the book because no matter what you pay people and how great the environment the manager/leader is the X factor on successful teams.

High school cross country meets are a perfect example of how creating a winning team rather than high performance individuals is how they win races. Running is an individual sport for sure but races like cross country change the rules by the team scoring and strategy. The bigger races recognize the developmental differences of the runner and allow kids and coaches to position kids in races where their talents and abilities will be best matched up with the competition.

The varsity races are designed to pit a team's best runners against the best competition. The race is not won by the fastest runners rather the team with the lowest overall score of the top 5 runners. The junior varsity and open races are just as important to the kids and the developmental aspect of the program which is why their results are just as important to the team.

Winning cross country coaches emphasize one aspect more than any other: getting the kids to run together. If you get a chance to watch a meet or race watch the number of kids on the same team that come in together. The kids run together in practice so they know who they need to run with on race day to have their best race. The kids always seem to push their peers and the pace at just a level below puking or passing out and then hold on until they can see the finish line when they literally throw down the hammer and give it their all.

The cool thing is everyone does the same thing at the end of the race.

They even finish stronger and faster than they ran at the beginning of the race. As the kids in the middle realize the race may have already been won minutes ago they know that every person they pass at the end could mean the difference in how their team performs even if their individual performance is well behind the fastest runners.

Creating that level of commitment, intensity and teamwork is not something that just happens. It requires great coaching and building leaders at all levels of the team. The best teams realize that greatness is more about effort of the team than the success of a few talented players.

One of the best programs that I've seen consistently apply this concept is Milton High School just north of Atlanta. The head coach Andy Car (an elite runner in his own right) has led the program for well over 10 years. What I respect most about the program is that Milton and Andy have a no cut policy on the cross-country team.

They typically have over 160 kids on the team each year show up on the first day of practice. At the end of the year they typically have even more kids. The kids struggle through the summer heat and humidity of Atlanta, Georgia. I've watched my oldest son literally pass out in a race it was so hot and humid. Why in those conditions would that many kids join the team? Because they want to be a part of a winning team and will put in the work and effort to earn the respect of their teammates.

Shortcuts and lack of discipline are just things the kids don't tolerate among themselves. The kids set the pace, reinforce the discipline and recognize their friends on race day for their effort and progress. The values of the team aren't just something written on a wall. It's what has driven the culture from an average team to one of the best programs in the state.

At the end of the year awards banquet the real successes are highlighted when the coaches recognize how much the kids have improved over the year. The aspect of personal growth and its impact on the team has never been more tangible when the kids go wild for the kids that showed the most improvement.

There isn't another sport that I'm aware of that has done a better job of creating winning teams by focusing on the improvement of everyone rather than just the contributions of the best players. Running together is the key to creating that positive tension that recognizes effort and rewards the progress of the team.

Take a few minutes before moving on to think about your team. You may want to blame your middle and low performers for their lack of interest, motivation and performance but aren't you as the manager responsible for the success of your team? If you're going to win don't you need everyone on the team pulling together and playing all out? If you said yes and believe that to be true then you are the problem and you are the solution.

<u>Where you are today is just a moment in time. How people are performing is just a reflection of how they've been treated, what they believe, and how inspired they are about what they're doing.</u>

Change the way they see themselves and their connection with the team and you can see the change in their behavior and performance over night. It's not skills or abilities that keep teams from winning rather their attitudes and sense of connection to a goal that determines their outcomes.

One morning I met with a young guy that was off the charts on intelligence, work ethic and accomplishments. He had his law degree, worked for one of the top consulting firms, and took a job with a large bank based in the southeast so he could be home at night to help raise his family. His boss at the bank had created such a toxic environment that instead of building this young guy up to his potential he told him he was a middle performer. It didn't take long for the young guy to take another job in a very highly regarded firm. His old boss was fired six months later. My guess is the boss was the middle performer.

The key here is a middle or low performing boss can pollute an entire team so when you see a trend look to the manager as the reason why!

As I talked about these definitions in our programs I always reminded the group that these can change as quickly as you can change a manager or leader. Put an energetic leader in a center or work station and watch performance go through the roof. Put a manager that's no longer inspired in the same environment and watch the performance plummet.

Early on, we learned that managers were shredding their people by working them without any sense of interest and appreciation. To get this to change we knew a critical element of our success was giving the managers the tools, training and recognition to make this Job One in the culture shift. They didn't realize it then but teaching the managers to recognize their people and show appreciation for the work that their teams were doing was the most impactful part of the program.

These managers had been groomed by their managers and in many cases, they weren't a great role model for creating winning teams. The managers that were quickest to adopt the new mindsets were the managers that became their future leaders.

Middle Challenge questions...

✓ Is your middle skewed by individuals or teams?

✓ Is the middle environmental or attitudinal?

✓ Are there "events" that made the middle more defined?

✓ Is the middle created by social groups or norms?

 <u>Bottom Line:</u> The single biggest factor in winning is the manager and leader. I refer to this dynamic countless times in the book because no matter what you pay people and how great the environment the manager/ leader is the X factor on successful teams.

The Social Influence of Teams

If I gave you $100,000 to bet on 3 individuals who would you put your money on?

The first individual is Brian. He's 30 lbs. overweight and says he's going to lose it this year. He's 40 years old and put on 30 lbs. over the past 10 years. He was an athlete in high school but now has a wife, 3 kids, and has a big job where he's required to travel a lot. He's a pragmatic individual and figures that he only needs to lose a fraction of a percent or .08 pounds a day for 365 days.

The second individual is Frank. He's 60 years old and just got a poor health diagnosis from his family doctor. He was told that if he doesn't change his diet and get more exercise that he'll need surgery or worse. He has a family history of heart attacks and strokes so no surprise that he would have to battle the same effects from the gene pool. His goal is to work out an hour a day, five days a week for a year. After he quickly calculates the time he realizes there's 168 hours in a week so working out five hours a week is really only 2.9 percent of the time.

The third individual is Kathy, a 40-year-old mom of three kids that signs up for Ironman Florida. She has been a consistent face in the gym for years but has never done anything more than run some 10k races and ridden 50 miles a few times with her friends. She did swim as a kid and still swims with the masters program but mostly to keep the weight off and see her friends. The Ironman is a 2.4 mile swim, 112 mile bike and capped off with a 26.2 mile marathon. The event is known as the single hardest one day event in sports. The race must be completed in less than 17 hours with the majority of the athletes taking between 12 – 15 hours to finish. To complete her goal, she's going to need increase her workouts from 5 hours a week to 15-20 hours a week. She admits she has no idea what she got talked into so gets a coach to guide her training.

Based on the above information we'll give you $100,000 and let you pick who you think will achieve their goal. If they achieve their goal you get to keep the cash but if they lose you lose. They don't know you're watching or betting on them. They don't win anything special or different for accomplishing their goal.

Who would you put your money on? Who has the highest likelihood to sustain the necessary discipline to achieve their goal? To improve your chances of winning the money my recommendation wouldn't be to measure the improvement gap but rather to compare the success rate based on others attempting the same goal.

It's time to place your bet!

Now let's introduce some information that may change your thought process.

Studies show that well over 80% of people starting weight loss programs have stopped within 30 days. Said another way, Brian has a whopping 20% chance of reaching his goal weight. Based on experience there's a real chance that at the end of the year he might have put on more weight.

Frank's chances are even worse with studies showing that 90% of people suffering heart attacks and heart surgery are back to their unhealthy habits in 18 months. Getting healthy even when the risks are staring people right in the face has only a 10% chance of success.

Surprisingly the data shows that 70% of people signing up for Ironman races go on to complete the race. That number is staggering knowing that the average person has to train upwards of 15–20 hours a week for over 8 months to prepare for a race.

Now who do you want to bet your $100,000 on? Where's your best chance of success and winning the cash? When you look even closer at the statistics you realize much of what people say they're going to do never is accomplished. Behavioral economists even have a term for it, it's called the "Say-Do-Gap." We say one thing but do something else. Oh and it gets better. We rationalize and justify our decisions for not doing it with other behaviors that also have names like "aversion to extremes," "the decoy effect" and "status motivation."

These are personal challenges but in the corporate world when leaders and employees are paid for results the outcomes aren't much better. According to a number of corporate studies only 20% of corporate initiatives and teams achieve their goals and true potential. This is referenced in the books titled *Positive Intelligence* by Shirza Chamine and *The Behavior Breakthrough* by Steven Jacobs.

The truth about change, habits and goals is that they are hard, require discipline and the likelihood of achieving the goal is lower than most people assume.

If you were one of the individuals how do you think you would do? Better than some random individual off the street? Nice try but that's what everyone thinks and it too has a name called "confirmation bias!"

If I were going with the greatest chance of winning the $100,000 I'm going to be betting on Kathy, that 40-year-old mom of three that just signed up for her first Ironman. Without ever having met her but knowing hundreds of other aspiring and accomplished Ironman triathletes, the reason why I'll always bet on them is you don't sign up for an Ironman without incredible motivation. Where that motivation came from is unique and every triathlete has their own story but I have yet to meet anyone that signs up for an Ironman and doesn't do it.

Based on extensive behavioral research conducted on the success rate of individuals who achieve their goals three elements need to be present for the change to occur.

1. It must be a personal goal.

2. There must be emotional commitment.

3. There must be constant focus.

These three elements are grounded in every 12-step program, behavioral change design and weight loss program known to man.

But if it is so simple, why is there such a high failure rate when people attempt some seemingly pretty easy and even life-extending goals? And why does a 40-year-old mom of three have a better chance of success at completing the hardest single day sporting event compared to somebody losing 30 lbs or working out five hours a week?

Throughout the book we explore the power of aspirational goals versus corporate or mandated goals and why one works so well and the others fail to get adopted or achieved. Moving the Middle is all about what works and what doesn't not only in the corporate world but in your personal life.

Behind all of man's greatest achievements is an aspirational goal and desire to be great or do great things. Tap into that force and you can move the world. Fail to ignite those aspirations and fail to realize your potential as a manager, a teacher, a parent, and as a team member.

This photo is of a good friend's beautiful wife. She had recently lost her leg but not her aspirational goal of being great! The beauty of the photo is that her friends knew the importance of their support and their power of encouragement and belief.

Let's go back to that $100,000 bet one more time. The mom aspires to be great. She aspires to inspire her kids to do amazing things. She doesn't see all the obstacles in front of her feet, only the finish line and that photo of crossing it together with her family. She never considers the training as punishment or torture; it's just what her coach told her she needs to do to achieve her goal. Her progress becomes more fuel for the fire and her social influences that surround her at the pool, track and on the bike only reinforce her desire, commitment, and resolve.

The social influence from her environment, teams, colleagues and family have an even greater impact on the outcomes than the goals themselves. Try losing 30 lbs. while you're traveling for business or during the holidays. It's brutal and the probability of success close to none!

Extensive clinical research has been done on the effect of social influences on individual behavior and it clearly points to the fact that we are products of our environment. Friends or spouses quit smoking and the likelihood that others in the group or marriage will quit smoking. Friends join Weight Watchers and their likelihood of losing weight together goes up. Friends take up working out and their friends begin to exhibit the same behavior.

The reason so many people do Ironman races isn't because it's something they've always wanted to do. Rather, it's the social influences of the group. The same holds true of the tattoos, the Ironman logoed clothes and car stickers.

Promote the right social influences on the team and you'll naturally speed up the adoption rate of the right behaviors, beliefs, and attitudes.

The same holds true for health, exercise programs, and performance improvement plans. The social influences are just as critical to your success as the skills and your plans for achieving your goals.

In a counterintuitive way, Kathy has the greatest advantage when we better understand her environmental factors. Welcome to one of the greatest paradoxes in human behavior: the principles of Moving the Middle.

Middle Challenge questions...

✓ What are the goals of your programs?

✓ What's the success rate of your goals and that of your team?

✓ Are your individual and team goals aspirational or mandated goals handed down from corporate?

✓ How can you infuse your programs with positive social influences?

✓ What is your team's emotional commitment to its goals?

Bottom line: Behind all of man's greatest achievements is an aspirational goal and desire to be great or do great things. Chances are that aspirational goal emanated from the positive influences of a group of like-minded individuals.

The Value of Building Strong Employee Brands

If I said Livestrong, what color, product and cause comes to mind?

If I said the Three-Day Walk, what color and cause comes to mind and how would you describe it?

How about the Ironman?

The Sweet 16?

The Super Bowl?

The Masters?

The Olympics?

Each of these brands has created such a strong awareness and emotion attached to them that they attract millions of participants and fans to experience their events.

The yellow wrist bands connected to Livestrong became one of the most recognized symbol for cancer support ever created.

The Three-Day Walks–and their pink-clad zealots–are legendary among women and families impacted by breast cancer.

The Ironman is known for its memorable finishes with such a strong brand that some athletes do the race just to get the tattoo.

The NCAA men's college basketball tournament has such a strong brand that to fill out a bracket once the tournament teams are announced at the beginning of the tournament has become a spring tradition in most offices and social groups.

The Super Bowl each year generates record worldwide TV viewership by matching up the best two professional football teams in the country. Even though most years it's a lopsided game, the experience is recognized as one of the most celebrated sporting events in the world. So much so that the broadcast has become the annual launch of the greatest advertising campaigns.

The Masters golf tournament is the crown jewel of a sport that is the past time of the wealthy, elite and the older generations. Despite the shrinking popularity of the sport those who get a chance to go to the event are amazed to see the long lines of fans waiting to buy shirts, hats, and everything the Masters can put their logo on.

What is it about these brands that carries such a powerful identity that people behave differently because of their desire to be associated with them? Whatever the motivation it's enough to increase the value of a hat or shirt three times its normal price.

The marketers behind sporting events and raising funds for curing cancer know their success is based on creating an emotional connection to their brands. But how does this apply to employee brands?

When we launched the Five Star program to the field we weren't really sure how the employees and managers would respond. Was it something they would roll their eyes at or was it something they would aspire to become? Five Star designation was not new in any industry so there was a good chance it would backfire because the reps didn't believe in it. What we did know was that we had just put the biggest aspirational brand on a program we had ever launched.

The most important aspect in the program design was that employees and managers wanted to be recognized as Five Star. The designation of being Five Star was such a powerful distinction that the program was a success the minute it was launched.

When we launched the program after the pilot we had the employees and managers on video talking about what it meant to be Five Star. What they said on the videos transformed the way people felt about their jobs overnight. They talked about their pride, excellence, and delivering a great customer experience like Five Star hotels and restaurants.

One manager commented that it was the best thing the company had done in 28 years! Five Star was a very strong aspirational goal but to get and keep everyone emotionally engaged we knew we couldn't just start handing out stars as participation trophies. So we built on the success with Five Star by creating Four Star recognition.

Four Star actually reinforced the strength of Five Star and expanded the recognition beyond top performers to employees and managers who were consistently improving their performance.

As Five and Four Star grew the brands were used on everything from trophies and plaques to hats, shirts and backpacks. When we put Five Star on a jacket everyone wanted to know how they could get one. The aspirational energy that Five and Four Star created only worked because the recognition meant something to the achievers and their social network.

Do your people wear your branded shirts to the gym with your colors and logo on it?

Do they promote the brand and take pride in being part of a winning team outside the workplace?

Do you or your employees have your corporate brand tattooed on your arms or legs?

If given the opportunity would your employees buy clothes with your brand on it for themselves, family and friends? Your employees do it for brands like Nike, Adidas, and Under Amour because they want to be associated with what that brand represents.

Great brands are the result of positive experiences people have when they interact with the company or products. Marketing and advertising companies know the power of strong customer brands and invest incredible amounts of time, money, and resources to get the branding right so when the consumer sees the name they connect on an emotional level. Why don't companies with even more at stake make the same effort to do the same for their employee brands?

Employee branding is simple. <u>It's not what you do rather it's what you want your employees to aspire to that creates the best branding.</u>

While you're going through the branding process, build your concepts around the aspirational desires of how you want the middle performers to think, feel, and act.

When your employees see it and hear it will they aspire to be part of the brand?

If I were to see somebody else wearing a shirt with the logo or name, would I want to know how I could get the shirt?

Your employee brand is important and should reinforce your values, your commitment to being a leader and your customer focus.

Why is this central to your strategy and long-term success?

<u>Your employees are in effect your consumers and customers. If you want them to respond and build an affinity to your team and company, the employee brand has to evoke an emotional bond of trust, confidence, respect, inspiration, and aspiration.</u>

If you don't agree let me ask you a few questions.

What is the name of your last employee program? How about the program before that? Now if I were to ask your employees the same question, what would they tell me? More importantly, what would they say about it? Is that the brand that's designed to recognize top performers or has it become the brand for getting everyone in the company to aspire to improve, deliver and contribute more?

How many of these brands exist within your company and how often do they last? If it's the program-of-the-month club, let me assure you that by design your organization is diminishing its chances of ever creating an employee brand of any substance.

Start small and pilot everything, including your employee branding. If your middle isn't inspired and doesn't buy it, then try again. Your employees will tell you what you need to know if you'll just ask honestly, listen, and then take action.

Middle Challenge questions...

✓ Start with your current employee program branding. How many programs currently exist? When were they launched? What are people saying about it? How is it designed to make the middle feel?

✓ What's your history of success in employee programs? How long do they last? Why do you change them out?

✓ What is that aspirational desire that will become the golden thread of all your communications, training, and recognition?

✓ Are you wearing the shirt? Hat? Did you get the tattoo?

✓ How is the brand being reinforced?

✓ What would you like it to be and who on your team understands what you want and has experience marketing brands?

 Bottom Line: Employee programs are just as dependent on strong branding as consumer product development is dependent on strong branding.

CHAPTER 3

THE MOTIVATION

"If it's your desires that drive
your habits, then designing
recognition and reward systems
that reinforce those desires is the
key to changing your behaviors,
activities and results."

– The Power of Moving the Middle, Jack Spartz

The Power of Emotional Engagement

My nephew Emerson Spartz is a respected leader in the field of virality. Emerson is the founder of Mugglenet, Dose, OMG Facts and numerous other online based social networks. He has literally built a career on making things go viral and has given multiple Ted Talks on the subject. He has a saying that "emotions are the common denominator for getting things to go viral." If something isn't emotional there's no reason to share, discuss or engage in it.

We've tested his theory in many of our program designs and I believe he's right on! If you can get someone to laugh, cry, scream, or be amazed, your message or idea will be shared and will go viral. Hopefully for the good of your cause and not to generate negative implications.

If you were to read and apply only one principle from this book I would say that it's this: the extent to which you can change your business is the extent to which you can get and keep your employees emotionally engaged. What Emerson found in his study on virality, we also found in our program design; emotion is the common denominator of success in any change management initiative.

Our world is full of emotions driven by the latest news, trends, and beliefs. Your company and team is being driven by this same dynamic. When employees hear your company is in trouble the emotions of fear drive their beliefs and behaviors. The same is true when they hear business is growing, expanding or there's a chance the company is being sold.

The reason it's so important is that those emotions are at the heart and soul of expectations and how people perform. How your people feel directly links to how they will perform.

When you woke up this morning, do you remember looking in the mirror as you washed your face and telling yourself "just get by?" If your people or team are waking up and telling themselves to "just get by," that lack of emotional energy and commitment will make it almost impossible to change performance.

If you think pride doesn't matter, walk down to your local Marine recruitment office and listen to the recruiters talking about a career as a Marine. It's all about pride! "The few, the proud, the Marines." They don't say "its super hard, we don't pay that much and if you do make it through basic training it gets even more challenging." They focus on the aspirational goals of individuals who want to do something amazing and be part of a high-performing team.

The 1st and 2nd level managers are the most important people in Moving the Middle, engaging your frontline employees and changing cultures. Consultants say it is the leaders but if the company is bigger than a few hundred people, the leaders lose their influence on the culture because they are too far removed from the day-to-day to influence how people and teams feel, act, and behave.

Test the theory out and you'll come to appreciate the simple, honest truth in this statement. The leader sets direction but as soon as they get off the phone or step down from the stage, *how* things get done is entirely up to the managers, which is why gauging culture and engagement across a large-scale audience is meaningless.

Every team, every work center and every call center has a very distinctive personality and culture and it's always a reflection of the manager rather than the leader.

The underlying issue with corporate cultures is seen almost weekly when a company's employee does something that is so outrageous that it warrants time on the national news. United Air Lines leadership might say that their culture is customer-centric but when we see a guy being dragged off a plane violently, we realize it is entirely different in practice or operation.

Yes, as a leader you can create a culture of compliance that in normal circumstances will serve you well but the minute stress is added to the equation, your real culture comes forth and that's what becomes newsworthy. This works both ways but it's the manager that shapes the culture more than the leader.

Case in point…we made a trip to Austin, Texas to meet with a call center leader that had literally transformed the performance of the call center and we wanted to know how she did it.

The minute you walk into this center, you feel like you are walking into a festive environment rather than a stoic, stagnant customer care call center. Nothing about how this center operated was like how the others operated – and when I met the center leader, it made perfect sense. Every answer she provided to my questions about what she did and why she did it was centered on creating a great employee experience.

The typical call center had rows and rows of cubicles, sales boards, and managers walking around listening to client calls. Not this place. The center of the call center was wide open and center stage with everything from a red carpet, basketball goal to a spin wheel the size of the one used on the Wheel of Fortune. The cubicles were organized in a radius around the center stage and the walls were wallpapered with crazy art.

The energy level in the center was off the charts and the people weren't just excited about what they were doing, they were the best in the company. They had walls of fame that celebrated years of service, birthdays, and every other accomplishment that warranted recognition.

What we experienced was far from the culture of the core company which leads me back to a critical belief, theory, and reality… the manager is the most important link in the ability to change your culture.

When asked how she got the approval to do all this cool stuff in the center she looked at us and responded, "If I asked for permission it would have taken so long and would have been so watered down that it wouldn't have worked."

What a great insight from someone who knew how to get things done. Do it and ask for forgiveness later. It wasn't long after our visit that she was promoted to another role. Good for her, bad for the company. The strategy was never expanded beyond that center and the impact of this change agent was limited to another role outside of that organization.

If it had been up to me I would have used that call center as a laboratory for new ideas and leadership development and would have had every manager in the company spend a few days in the Austin center to learn directly from this leader.

Moving the Middle is all about creating the experience for your employees with the understanding that the manager is critical to your success.

Are there times that people aren't emotionally engaged when they have success? Sure, but they are few and far between. Everyone exhibits emotional engagement differently but without much effort you can walk into a retail store, small business, sales office or any other business and tell who's emotionally engaged and who's not. You can tell who's in and who's out.

You don't need surveys to find out which teams are unhappy and which ones don't want to leave at night. Your customers can tell as well, which is why it's so important to rethink the value in Moving the Middle in your organization. 60%–70% of all your transactions and interactions as a company are handled by your middle performers. Can you really afford to ignore this large of an employee population that services your customers?

The great news is that getting your people emotionally engaged doesn't have to cost you a dime and probably has the biggest ROI of any change management strategies. Compare the cost of the rational levers to the inspirational performance levers. We think it's time the inspirational levers had as much thought and energy applied to them as has been invested in getting the rational elements right.

Middle Challenge questions...

✓ What are your performance levers?

✓ What are the costs of each lever and how does it impact performance?

✓ What are the levers being used the most and why?

✓ What are the levers that aren't being used but offer the greatest opportunity?

✓ How can you get expectations, training and adoption of the lesser used levers?

✓ Who needs to be on your team to understand the issue and develop the plan?

<u>Bottom Line:</u> The reason emotions are so important is that they are at the heart and soul of expectations and how people perform. How your people feel directly links to how they will perform.

How Goals Really Impact Performance

There are three key questions when considering the strategy for employee goals.

1. What's the gap?

2. What's fair?

3. And what's realistic in terms of improvement?

The problem with goal-setting isn't the goals but the number of goals teams, individuals and companies are pursuing.

S.M.A.R.T. (Specific, Measurable, Achievable, Relevant, and Time-Sensitive) goals are less effective than a To-Do List when the number of goals exceeds the ability to manage all the necessary resources to keep them top of mind and on track.

The name for this dysfunction is goal diffusion. The number of goals becomes so large and in many cases conflicting that software companies have developed apps so people can list out all their goals and attempt to track their progress. The apps sound promising and I've tried a few of them myself but once the number of goals exceeds five, the human mind has a challenge even remembering them all which explains the term "goal diffusion."

Goal setting has become so embedded in the world of sports, diets, health and corporate planning that it's common for most people to be pursuing numerous career and personal goals that are in direct conflict with one another. Spending more time with the family, spending more time in the gym to get healthy, and getting ahead at work by working more hours are all great goals that are in direct competition with each other because they all demand the same resource for success: time.

Every New Year's Day, millions of like-minded individuals sit down to write out the resolutions that will make them better, nicer, and more productive people and help them achieve better lives during that calendar year. Sadly, the latest statistics on resolution goal achievement show an 80–90% failure rate.

If people setting New Year's resolutions have only a 10–20% chance of success what do you think the success rate is when managers set goals for their employees at the beginning of the year?

I always bet against achievement of corporate goals because it's rare that they're realistic, have the necessary momentum behind them, and have the buy-in and commitment from the front-line employees to actually deliver the necessary effort to achieve them. Also in play is the fact that goals that are devoid of emotion are devoid of potential and achievement.

If companies knew what could change behavior and results, this outdated process would have been scrapped years ago.

Here are several principles I have learned about goals and impact on performance.

- Proximity is key! Programs that establish goals that are within reach outperform all other programs.

- Belief matters! Programs succeed because consistently meeting these goals builds employee confidence, skills and self-efficacy.

- Making the goal personal, creating emotional commitment, and providing constant focus are critical to their long-term success.

- It turns out that big-stretch goals that have little chance of being achieved are no better than having no goals at all.

- The social influence of the group is key in driving emotional beliefs, adoption and changing behaviors to achieve results.

If results are a byproduct of activities, behaviors and habits, without the emotional commitment from the participant the goal has the same 10-20% chance of succeeding.

If the goal is designed to drive individual performance, then it's important to understand the impact on various goal/incentive/recognition systems. There are five basic goal systems that cover 90% of all programs.

1. Self-selected

2. Improvement-Over-Self

3. Best-in-Class

4. Plateau Level

5. Universal

Which do you think are the most effective and engaging?

The answer is based on where people are on the performance curve, the trend, and the potential for improvement. While you consider the options let me give you two things to consider. First, which goal system would you advocate for your family or those you love? Second, which goal system would you choose for yourself?

Change your answer?

The two that I have found to be most effective are Self-Selected goals and Improvement-Over-Self goals. The Best-in-Class goals are also important because they provide the appropriate recognition and tension on top performers to maintain their current performance levels

Improvement-Over-Self goals are the best at Moving the Middle because they create just the right amount of dynamic tension to keep employees engaged without making them stressed or demoralized. By using personal trends as the basis for goals, you can increase the level of the goals as performance and efficacy improves. It may not align with the traditional all or nothing incentive design, but it works far better.

When applying this approach to goal-setting in Five Star, each manager and employee had five separate metrics on which they could earn stars for achieving their Best-in-Class or Improvement-Over-Self goals. Every month, the goals reset themselves and every three months the targets were adjusted for seasonality and progress to make sure they maintained the right tension on the organization.

During the eight years the program operated, there were only two times that leaders decided to change the goals to utilize Universal goals. I'm glad they did because it gave us more insight and experience on how Universal goals impacted performance compared to improvement over self and best in class goals.

The first attempt using Universal goals was tested for six months. After three months, the client realized the negative impact it was making on their business but was locked in to the changes because of communications made to the field. It was a $900,000 error in judgement and almost shut down the Five Star program.

The leaders felt that the Universal goals were simpler to understand and rewarded their top performers so they made the case for the changes.

They rolled out the Universal goals and then sat back and watched their employees' productivity soar. I didn't understand what was happening until I saw the quality metric go down. The balanced scorecard of Five Star created just the right tension on the metrics to insure they moved together and not in opposite directions. By making the change the organization changed the dynamics and resulted in inflated productivity scores and a bigger problem in quality.

Quality was being sacrificed for speed and resulted in the need to send technicians back out to clients' homes to fix issues multiple times. After six months of Universal goals the changes were scrapped and replaced with Best-in-Class and Improvement-Over-Self goals.

Universal goals were tested a second time when they were offered in addition to the standard program rules. There was absolutely no lift, no improvement and it resulted in paying people more for the jobs that they were already doing.

The folks in finance saw the flaw in these changes when they ran the numbers but like most bad ideas they had to live through the experience to prove the case.

The objective should always be to have employees select and even aspire to their own goals.

<u>Believing goals are attainable is always the first step in achieving them.</u>

I found a similar response when we rolled out Just Ask, the customer referral program, to the managers and technicians. Our team set the bar of two referrals a year per technician as a baseline goal and everyone said, "no problem, everyone can do that!" We could have jammed everyone and told them up front we needed two sold referrals a month to meet the business case obligations but to do that would have imposed our goals on them and reduced our chances of success.

Middle Challenge questions...

✓ Are there any ways to pilot the use of self-selecting goals?

✓ Do you have data to look back at the success rates of different goal strategies, so you can learn from direct experience?

✓ Is there a way to test the different goal systems at the manager and team levels?

✓ How many individuals are achieving the goals?

✓ Is that an indication of progress and success or the lack of buy-in and motivation?

One of the key success factors in establishing goal systems is designing them with the expectation that everyone should believe they can achieve the goal.

Going back to the goal of completing an Ironman... how many people do you think would plunk down a check for $700 if they didn't believe they could complete the race? My guess is very few. Ironman understood this factor as it built its brand and developed the tagline "anything is possible" to instill that belief in their athletes.

 Bottom Line: Believing goals are possible is always the first step in achieving them.

Raising the "BAR"

Don, a close friend of mine suffered a broken neck while out on a training ride a few years back. Don was riding his bike in the North Georgia mountains when he was struck by a car. The driver of the car was in a jeep and made a U-turn in the middle of the road. He didn't see Don coming in the opposite direction flying down the road on his road bike. It all happened in an instant. As Don describes it, he went right through the front passenger window and ended up in the lap of the Jeep passenger.

If the accident happened to any of the other 50 plus athletes we trained with they would have ended up paralyzed or dead. Don was by far the strongest physically and mentally to survive the accident but even weeks later he looked terrible.

After leaving the hospital in one of those big bulky body braces, Don began to think of how the accident would change his life. Would he ever ride or run again? Triathlons? Golf? Initially progress and healing were slow but as Don got stronger he realized his accident was a gift and an opportunity to share his experience with others in a positive way. Amazingly less than a year later he signed up, trained for and ran the NYC Marathon while raising money for the Christopher Reeve foundation.

How does lying in bed hoping you'll be able to walk one day turn into signing up and training for a marathon less than a year later? There's no science to prove this but our experience showed that the right activities and behavior drive progress which produces improvement which is its own reward and motivation. <u>The first rule of motivation is that if it is not intrinsic, it will always require constant feeding and attention.</u>

In the book *The Power of Habit* by Charles Duhigg, the author states that "desire is what best sustains a habit." Don's intrinsic motivation to help others is what got him up out of bed training for a marathon despite all the setbacks and challenges he faced.

Fortunately, you don't have ask employees to train for and run marathons but the principles behind motivation and meaning are the same if you're asking for an increased level of commitment and discretionary effort.

My nephew Johnny, a great student and an average athlete, experienced this principle first hand in high school. He always aspired to be a great athlete while participating in swimming, Ironkids triathlons and every other organized sport. As he got older, because of his asthma and diminishing skills he realized that there were fewer and fewer sports he could participate in because of the level of competition.

By high school Johnny's team sport options had been narrowed down to swimming. His parents had a rule that the kids had to be involved in at least one sport throughout the school season so swimming was it.

Johnny was more of a "participant" on the team rather than a leader in the pool before the summer of his junior year. Johnny was a late bloomer and that short, asthmatic kid started to reap the benefits of puberty and a massive growth spurt. The coach noticed the change and had seen something in his swimming that got them both excited about the year ahead. Johnny's size was coupled with long arms, flexible ankles and a desire to be great. Despite growing up with asthma, he had an incredible ability to hold his breath and propel himself on his back under water while kicking, a big advantage to doing a great back stroke.

By the time the high school swim team kicked off his junior year, that small advantage created small wins, increased desire, and that kid from the middle was now winning races and a top performer. As Johnny's motivation grew, his belief in himself grew into what he could accomplish.

While visiting Houston that season, his mom (my sister) asked if I wanted to watch Johnny swim in a meet that evening. Over the years I had watched Johnny play soccer, basketball, Ironkids and swim and I always hoped he was going to be a smart kid because sports weren't his strength.

I went to the swim meet to spend time with my sister and see how Johnny was progressing. Johnny crushed the field. When it was over, I couldn't get over the transformation. My sister pointed to the coach and said that it never would have happened if it wasn't for him. <u>To see something special in a person and inspire them is one of the most beautiful gifts of life.</u>

The coach knew the importance of meaning in motivation and used Johnny's desire to be great to fan the flames of his desire, effort, and improvement. Johnny went on to become one of the top back-strokers in Texas, swam at the collegiate level at Purdue and even swam in the Olympic Trials.

In retrospect Johnny could have easily slipped through the cracks like so many other people do in life, never realizing their full potential. Yes, it required an incredible amount of work to go from the middle to the best but with the right intrinsic motivation, his progress was the fuel for his improvement, discipline, and work ethic.

My oldest brother Jimmy suffered two massive strokes eight years ago that left him paralyzed on his left side and his speech seriously impaired. Initially he struggled with what the surgeons and specialists told him. They said, "you shouldn't be here. The strokes you suffered were so massive that there's very few individuals that have overcome those odds."

Jimmy wasn't a fan of the wheelchair so one day he said, "no more" and put the wheelchair in the closet and began to walk with a cane. With progress and time Jimmy put the cane next to the wheelchair in the closet and said, "no more" to his crutch. He's not fast but as you see him pivoting off his left side to move forward you don't know if you should cheer or cry. He didn't stop there. He decided that being stuck in the house waiting for rides was for the birds so he relearned how to drive and got his driver's license.

What Don, Johnny and Jimmy share is an inherent determination to own life and not let life own them. Don wanted to inspire, Johnny wanted to achieve, and Jimmy just didn't want to miss out on all the fun of life and become a prisoner of his paralysis.

After facing such massive obstacles and setbacks, why didn't they give up and take the easy way out? Why should you, your team or your company be any different?

Ask yourself how you've achieved success. My guess is that you have had a coach or colleague who has inspired and motivated you to think, feel, and act differently and to believe in yourself. If you want to be remembered by your team when they move on, it's the ability to bring out the best in all your people that is always valued above all else.

This ability to bring out the best in people is critical with motivation and the middle. Different performance groups respond to different stimuli and

<u>it's up to you to make sure you're giving each group the proper inspiration to maximize their motivation.</u>

Motivating a team or work group seems like a simple task until you launch a few programs and they fail right before your eyes.

You ask what happened. We gave them an opportunity to make more money. Why didn't it work?

If your employees don't care, commit or believe nothing changes.

When you assess your programs that succeed and fail, what was the noticeable difference?

<u>The underlying thread for failure in corporate initiatives is the lack of motivation impacting engagement and adoption.</u>

<u>Was there a strong WHY or HOW?</u>

Maybe the WHAT is generally understood, but you'll find the WHY and HOW are the real drivers of success. Without a sense of commitment and engagement, the motivation and discretionary effort are going to be missing from the equation.

Over the years there's been an emerging science called behavioral economics that helps us understand what drives motivation. Many principles are baked into the motivation of our daily lives. Once understood, the principles can be incorporated into your future program design.

Can motivation be measured? Can it be consistently applied? Can it be compared from employee to employee? What's a predictable way to gauge motivation?

All great questions and the answer is no, no, no, and no.

If there's no way to measure motivation, then how do we know if employees are engaged and motivated?

We break this down in the framework of **think - feel - do**. How you think drives how you feel and how you feel impacts what you do. In this way, you can measure motivation that's displayed as behaviors, activities, and results and not expressed as an emotional score.

Motivation is emotional, not rational.

Athletes who train for 20+ years at the highest level in relative obscurity to go to the Olympics have an emotional commitment. It's not a rational decision. It's rarely an individual motivation and commitment to the goal that achieves massive success.

We interviewed individuals in low performance quadrants and replayed the tapes of how they viewed their jobs, boss, customers and career. The comments were logical and rational about their perceived effort, meaning and the purpose they felt towards their contribution.

As we listened to the tapes of middle and top performers, we noticed a marked difference in their beliefs and attitudes towards these same questions.

Individuals in high-performing teams responded to the questions with more of a 'we' than 'me' attitude towards their jobs and purpose. The higher performing teams had a sense they were part of something bigger and greater than their individual performance. This was in stark contrast to individuals in low performing teams who had a sense of isolation and independence.

It's not a perfect math equation and it will never find its way into any physics book but what I believe we uncovered was a better indicator of future performance and motivation than all those employee engagement surveys combined. Write it down and test the theory on your own team and company.

$$M = B + A + R$$

<u>The sum of your Behaviors + Activities + Results equals your Motivation. An easy way to remember this is: to raise the BAR on motivation measure your behaviors, activities and results.</u>

We may never understand the source of motivation but I believe if you track the key activities, behaviors, and results, you can measure it.

People can say what they want about how they feel, what's important to them, and what they say they are going to do but it rarely comes to pass unless the sum of their activities, behaviors, and results drive the motivation for change. When you assess your potential for change, understand the motivation to change by measuring the trajectory of the activities, behaviors, and results and you'll have all the data you need to understand your likelihood to succeed.

Bottom Line: The key to remember is that high performers in both groups had connected with an emotional purpose, while the lower performers connected through a rational explanation.

The Value of Cash in Recognition

As a parent, I offered cash as a pay for performance incentive with my kids when they were playing sports. Early on improvement was easy and I liked to think I was teaching my kids this great lesson rewarding them with cash incentives for their improvement. When improvements came easy it sounded great but when they came less frequently, the kids resented the deal and felt I was being unfair.

Cash incentives are like diets, they sound good and look easy but work less than 20% of the time. As the effort to improve becomes more difficult, the value of the incentives goes down. What I experienced with the kids is the same response we got when offering cash incentives to employees.

<u>What we found was when offering cash as a form of incentive, the first two questions that most people ask are "how much is it?" and "is it worth it?"</u> Face it, if your employees passed sixth grade math they know the value probably better than you.

Now let me ask you what's the value of improvement to you and the company? Not all jobs offer incentives to drive improvements, but many do so it's important to think in terms of the value of that incremental effort and production.

✓ When considering cash incentives if you doubled your incentives would you double your revenue or production?

✓ How much is the incentive in relationship to the rest of their earnings?

✓ When you offer more cash compensation is it something you can sustain or is it just to close a gap?

✓ Are you planning to pay out cash incentives to your entire organization?

✓ The middle performers?

✓ How much of a lift do you expect for your cash incentive?

✓ Is it just a top performer program designed only to engage the few for a short period of time?

✓ If so, are you doing yourself a favor next month or next quarter if you can't offer the incentive?

When you monetize the award value of achievement the calculative nature of your employees reinforces that it's more profitable to work a few hours overtime in a week than to be a high achiever.

The biggest challenge when offering cash as the incentive is that cash becomes considered as part of the compensation package.

Let's say one year you offer a lot of extra incentives and your people build it into their income expectations but the following year that budget is being spent on other parts of the business. Your employees will react a lot like my kids did. They will resent you when the offer is eliminated or when achieving the goals becomes increasingly difficult.

Playing games with your employee compensation is one of the worst sins a leader can commit in business because it tends to undermine their long-term success for short term wins.

Resentment regarding compensation leads to lower productivity, low engagement and high turnover. What feels good in the moment has long term effects that can cost more in the end.

If cash isn't the answer what are the other options?

One strategy that we tapped into heavily was recognition and the emotional residue of its effect on individuals pursuing a goal or having achieved its reward. Take the Ironman for example. What drives a person to pay a $700 entry fee, train 20 hours each week for several months, wake up every morning at 5:00 am to swim-bike-run (aka train)?

One of my friends described the dream of crossing the finish line with her kids and that image propelled her through a year of endless workouts. Another friend always wanted to hear the famous words, "You are an Ironman."

The finish line to an Ironman is pretty impressive and as close to an Olympic moment that most people will ever experience. The recognition Ironman has created around finishing a race is such a powerful force that people tattoo their bodies with the Ironman logo and or the distance of 140.6 miles. Talk about emotional residue!

The recognition extends past the finish line and becomes a symbol like no other I've ever encountered. Show me one other achievement (other than the Olympics) that has created such an emotional connection to achievement that participants want to permanently display it as a badge or medal for all to see.

Recognition is pretty powerful stuff if you get it right!

How is recognition built into your employee experience?

When did you literally cry, smile, or gush at the last recognition you received at work?

Don't be ashamed. Be thankful that you received something so priceless that to put a cash value on it reduced its intrinsic value to you.

Not long before a close friend of mine resigned from her job, she was called up to receive a special award. The leader brought the individual up on stage and recognized her for working long hours and through incredible obstacles to deliver a new product.

She walked onto the stage with her head spinning knowing that this presentation was being watched by employees all over the world. The feeling of "this is the biggest day of my life" came over her. She made it on stage and barely noticed the statements being made about her efforts as she was overwhelmed with the moment. The leader shook her hand and took a photo with her and then handed her a plaque and envelope. She breathlessly whispered, "thank you," as she smiles from ear to ear. She accepted the award and walked back to her seat. When she got back to her row, her colleagues slapped her on the back saying, "that was awesome." Midway into the next recognition speech, she opens the envelope and sees a debit card for $100.

Are you kidding me?

Her mind was screaming as she calculated the countless hours of discretionary effort and unpaid overtime it took to pull off that little miracle her leader just told everyone about.

She thought the envelope contained a personal note from the leader thanking her but what she got was a cheap substitute for honest and sincere appreciation.

Instead of reinforcing the moment, they tried to place a value on it. I'm sure they thought they were being very generous based on their budget or some other financial parameters set up to control costs.

When she got home that night, she was embarrassed and didn't even tell her significant other about the recognition. Her effort and accomplishment were only worth $100.

Over the course of many years, we learned a simple principle that needs to be tattooed on the forehead of every corporate leader in America: keep your cash, it's not worth it. The moment was especially lost in the missed expectation surrounding cash vs. public recognition and personal appreciation.

Compensation is one thing you don't want to ever mix with inspiration. If you do, you devalue the intrinsic motivation which is the reason your team did it in the first place.

Recognition is a powerful performance lever in driving performance and change in an organization. It signals significance, relevance, and shows appreciation in formal and informal settings. It creates positive press and a means for sharing stories. It provides a culture, atmosphere, and tools to show leaders and managers how to lead with a positive attitude.

Below is a sample Recognition Scorecard to help you list all your programs and better understand what values and priorities your programs are reinforcing. The scorecard highlights your strengths but also your opportunities when it comes to improving the performance and engagement of your team and company.

Creating a balanced approach to your recognition strategy signals that the importance of continuous improvement and progress are as critical to the long-term success of the team as are the results you're experiencing today.

As you review each metric priority, list what reinforcement "currency" you are using to make it tangible, visible and promotable. If you're using certificates for training, challenge your team to ask how are we using this to reinforce our values and priorities? If you've limited your recognition to cash incentives and only for the top performers, step back and ask: how is this impacting the other 90% of the team or company? Is it a good thing?

The Recognition Scorecard is only a starting point and should reflect and align with your business priorities.

Recognition/ Metrics	Productivity	Sales	Customer Satisfaction	Training/ Certification	Values	Team Results
Behaviors						
Activities						
Results						
Improvement Over Self						
Best in Class						
Top Performer						
Frequency						
$/Value						

Middle Challenge questions...

✓ Recognition is the positive **reinforcement** for those activities, behaviors, and accomplishments aligned with the corporate values and goals.

✓ Instill leaders at all levels of the organizations with the understanding that recognition (reinforcement) is the most powerful force in instilling a high-performance culture and leading a culture shift.

✓ Expand the reach, frequency, and tangible recognition (reinforcement) of employees and managers living the values, goals, behaviors, activities, and results.

✓ Celebrate and recognize (reinforce) those giving and receiving the recognition.

✓ Instill frequent, immediate, and genuine praise as routine to create a sustainable high-performing, high-touch culture.

✓ Establish baselines of engagement and performance to track, analyze, and monitor improvement areas

✓ Use employee recognition measurements as a barometer for engagement, attitude, and culture status.

<u>Bottom Line:</u> If you want something to be repeated, reinforce it with recognition. Build your recognition programs around your values, priorities, and the behaviors, activities and results that shape success in your business.

Progressive Equity

If you've ever been in a busy call center you know it's one of the most dynamic and challenging work environments ever created. Inbound or outbound it doesn't matter... it's crazy! Managers are jumping from call to call working with reps trying to resolve issues, process hundreds of calls an hour and meet their hourly targets.

In a way it's the perfect human performance lab because you can test almost any engagement strategy in the course of an hour, a day or a week and determine its effectiveness.

Despite this incredible lab environment where you would think managers and leaders would be open to new ideas and trying new approaches, what we experienced was the complete opposite. What they were doing they had been doing for years. The willingness to try new ideas was blocked by leaders who thought they had all the answers and repeated all the same mistakes.

The beliefs of the leaders were reinforced in their designs making it almost impossible to question their results until they got in a crisis situation or left the company. What the leaders didn't know was hurting them and their ability to make their numbers.

The problem in a nutshell was the client was only getting performance from a very limited group of people and to make their numbers they were having to pay an increasing amount of money to get the same performance. The middle was completely disengaged as evidenced by the lack of effort and results when new incentive programs were launched.

In truth the call centers operated like crack houses with the performers requiring more and more stimulus for the same response. The problem with this approach was it was creating a negative reinforcement loop and not a positive one in the environment. What started out as a $2.00 blitz incentive per sale became $10.00. A blitz day incentive of $100.00 became $200.00 for the same performance a year later. The escalating payouts were resulting in the same or lower performance.

What we learned is that the impact on employee motivation of giving more money is very brief (if there is any impact at all) because it's spent as quickly as they earn it. The reason for this is that 69 percent of Americans have less than $1,000 in their savings account while 34 percent have nothing saved at all based on a survey done in November 2016, by GOBankingRates.

The cash was giving the few people that were winning a quick dopamine hit but since there was no promotability or social currency linked back to the incentive no one was talking about it. When no one talks about what they got from their incentives the impact is contained and limited.

What the leaders failed to understand using cash as their incentive currency was what the airlines have been doing for decades. The point system leveraged the power of progressive equity in their programs and the cool awards created social currency, status motivation, and the promotability of the awards.

Progressive equity was a term we developed to describe the accumulation of points or equity in incentive programs. Normally individuals start out in these programs and don't have many points or equity in the programs but as their equity grows it changes their engagement and commitment.

The airlines and credit card loyalty programs understand this and offer large sums of points to sign up creating the illusion of wealth in the program and what Behavioral Economists have termed "illusionary goal progress."

In the case of a business traveler they select an airline, a hotel and a car rental company based on who is offering the most points and where they have the greatest equity in their programs. This is despite the cost differences in rates which in many cases may be more than the points are worth.

The airlines realized years ago that if they could reward a customer with points towards a trip, hotels, or merchandise it would change the way customers think, feel and behave when booking flights. It became so successful that rental car companies and hotels all followed suit as they watched the results prove out year after year.

As the cumulative effect of points increases, we more fully understand the motivation (behaviors, activities and results) of individuals collecting and accumulating points. The more you collect the more vested you become in the program (and thus that company/brand/service).

As we sign up for these programs, it's typically not a big deal because we realize we will have to make numerous trips or accumulate points over a long period of time to earn any of the bigger awards. But as individuals achieve predetermined threshold levels, their behavior predictably changes resulting in higher levels of interest and engagement.

The more airline points we collect, the more these potential trips and upgrades make us feel differently towards the airlines, hotels, credit cards, etc. thus giving them more of our business.

The same principles that motivate travelers worked with my client's employees when they changed from using cash incentives to points-based programs. By recognizing behaviors, activities and results using points, the company could issue smaller increments more frequently to reinforce desired behavior while developing emotionally engaged employees.

The new approach emphasized building equity in programs vs. cash based incentives to drive performance. As the equity in the programs increased, the client was able to reduce the value of the payouts while getting better results and greater participation.

The real change in performance came when the client started using the point programs to incentivize middle performers to drive improvements. This group who had been neglected for years was now getting recognized for progress and improvements and guess what happened? Their performance improved so much that the client realized their greatest gains were coming from the middle performers.

When the company recognized them with even modest point rewards, they changed the way the middle performers thought about their jobs and felt about the company.

We were working in a call center in Macon, Georgia. The client was increasing their incentive payouts but complaining that the incentives weren't working any more. As my team analyzed the payouts we realized that more than 80% of incentives were going to 15% of their people.

Their top performer bias in the rules design was causing them to pay top performers increasingly more even though their sales were decreasing as a percentage.

By designing their incentive programs using cash they created a coin operated environment and escalated sales expenses that only generated a response with the sales reps that were already top performers. The middle performers not only didn't respond to the cash incentives, but found themselves in a toxic environment in the process.

The client agreed to changing the design and structure of their incentive programs and it had such a positive effect on their performance it was scaled to all the rest of the call centers in the company. The solution was to decrease the top performers payouts in cash and layer a point based incentive for improvement goals for everyone else. The program went on to operate for years because the middle was the group that was driving the greatest increases in revenue.

Another example of this was in a customer referral program that was using cash incentives for customer referrals. The employees said they wanted cash. The managers from the field echoed this belief by adding they needed to increase the incentive payouts to improve engagement. The problem was the program was in crisis mode as referrals and revenue from the program were dropping off significantly year to year.

The client changed leadership of the program and informed the new leaders that their budgets would be cut by 25%. The new leader followed our advice by changing the cash incentives to points while reducing the point value of each referral.

During the transition we also changed the marketing and messaging around the program. In particular, in our periodic communications to employees we highlighted the trips and merchandise the employees could earn. Within a year the program had gone viral and was delivering double digit growth.

The cumulative value of the points had a bigger impact on engagement and performance over time and as the equity in the points grew the program grew faster. What we also realized was happening was that as one employee earned a big award with their points they were more willing to talk about it and promote it within their group. As the stories circulated, they triggered an emotional response throughout the company.

When people earned cash, it had limited social currency because it wasn't polite to brag about what you bought. Employees didn't feel that way about what they earned with their points as they openly shared what they were getting with their points as almost status motivation.

The awards were becoming so popular we launched an employee campaign called Share Your Story so employees could promote what they won with their points. The awards that they were winning were impressive and the stories became legendary throughout the company. The stories went viral as they were promoted on the company website and the employees earned recognition from their peers and social status for their stories.

Talk about an incredible turnaround and the power of progressive equity and the principles of behavioral economics to change the trajectory of a failing program.

Middle Challenge questions...

✓ What types of currencies are you using in your incentive programs?

✓ How are the awards being shared or discussed to create social currency?

✓ Is there any promotability to your awards to reinforce the winners?

 __Bottom Line:__ **If you're trying to change the dynamics of your incentives take a note from the playbooks of the industries that have made a science out of loyalty, engagement, and behavior change.**

Inspiration or Compensation

One of my favorite people and bosses of all time stood up in a presentation and asked the client what they were using their incentives for–inspiration or compensation? The client was spending over $20 million on cash-based incentives and from what we could tell they weren't working. By asking the question he nailed one of the most important aspects of incentives and recognition there is, are you using your incentives to generate inspiration or compensation?

It's easy to rationalize compensation but as you've gone through the stories I hope you realize it's inspiration and not compensation that changes behaviors, activities, and results.

You could have heard a pin drop as we sat around an oversized mahogany table in the client's boardroom. Their CEO had just asked whether we knew what people buy with their incentives. In the past we had given them reports on what they were getting with the points, but it was pretty high-level data. What the client wanted to know was exactly what my boss had asked 15 years earlier, were the incentives being used as inspiration or compensation.

Years later the CEO asked "what were people buying with the incentives they earned?" The question resulted in one of the most incredible studies on incentive spending behavior and its implication on engagement and performance. The study tracked participants for multiple years and analyzed what they earned and what they spent their incentives on using cash vs. points. The cash was on reloadable debit cards and the points were issued on an employee recognition platform funded by the client.

The group we analyzed exceeded 10,000 employees and the value of the awards was well in the tens of millions of dollars. There was no evidence of a study like this ever done before and what was so unique about it was that it was real life data and not some test created and operated in a laboratory. These were real life people with real life money and points making real decisions on how they were going to spend their incentives.

The reason this is so important is the data and results demonstrate which types of incentives were most effective.

Since we had thousands of participants, millions of dollars issued in incentives, and thousands of transactional data in spending behavior, we were able to compare a number of differences between cash and point-based programs. We were able to see how long people saved cash vs. points and the types of purchases made using the different currencies.

The employees earned on average anywhere from $100.00 to $500.00 a month in incentives. The client issued approximately $4.00 in cash for every $1.00 in points.

Since it helps to engage your brain before you learn something new let me challenge you with a few questions.

✓ What do you think was most effective?

✓ How well do you think people saved their cash-based incentives vs. points?

✓ What do you think people bought with their incentives using cash vs. points?

✓ What do you think was the average transaction value for cash and points?

The big winners from the cash based incentives were McDonald's, Wendy's, Burger King, Kentucky Fried Chicken, and convenience stores. Walmart did make the list but wasn't a top player.

- 55% of the cash transactions were less than $10.00 with the average transaction coming in at a little over $7.00.
- 75% of the cash transactions were less than $20.00.
- 92% of the cash transactions were less than $50.00.
- 3% of the cash transactions were greater than $100.00.

The title of the chapter was there for a reason. Inspiration or compensation? Yes, you can use cash as compensation for your incentives, but based on how your employees spend incentives, how much emotional residue do you think a Big Mac has on their inspiration and long-term behavior? My guess is the airlines used cash incentives early on and realized this same insight. If you're using cash as a source of motivation you better have deep pockets.

Based on the findings we quickly realized from the spending behavior of the participants why cash was such an ineffective motivator. <u>Motivation is all about aspiration and inspiration.</u> The "I can" and "I will" is the lifeblood of success in life. The problem with cash as the incentive was that the participants spent the money like coins in their pockets and as a result there was no sense of a special reward, no trophy value and no memory of the purchases to create the social currency, status motivation and desire to give the extra effort the next time an incentive was offered.

It's easy to see why so many of the people eligible to earn these incentives never engaged or applied extra discretionary effort for the money. If after a few months you have nothing to show for your efforts, you can easily rationalize not trying and not winning because it makes no difference in your life.

The points on the other hand had an inverse relationship in terms of savings and spending vs. the debit card.

- 2% of the points-based transactions were less than $10.00.

- 8% of the points-based transactions were less than $20.00.

- 48% of the points-based transactions were greater than $100.00.

People saved the points longer and spent them on bigger items that were more visible, tangible, and sociable. The average purchase value was over $400 despite the earning opportunities being substantially less. It took anywhere from 4 to 5 times as long to earn the same amount as people earning cash on debit cards so savings were even more difficult and deliberate.

The top purchases with points were big screen TVs, family vacations, golf clubs, bikes, concerts, flights, hotel rooms, and rental cars. People were using the points for big purchases and personal experiences. The more they saved the more engaged they became in the programs fueling a motivation in the middle performers we had never experienced before.

The study only confirmed what we knew for years but had needed proof to demonstrate: cash is compensation, it's rational and only has a limited ability to motivate people to put forth discretionary effort. If you want to inspire and motivate your middle performers save your money and use the principles and tools we discussed throughout the book to change how your employees look, think, and feel about their jobs.

Middle Challenge questions...

✓ Are you using incentives as compensation or inspiration?

✓ Have you created a transactional or aspirational culture of recognition?

✓ How are you using compensation and incentives to drive different behaviors and results?

✓ What is your understanding of the impact this is having on results?

✓ What is working and what needs to be adjusted? Why?

 Bottom Line: One of the most crucial principles in motivation is that it's not the value of the incentive but the importance and relevance of the recognition to the participant that is the best predicator of engagement.

CHAPTER 4

THE
MODELS

"True genius resides
in simplicity."

– Mozart

Progression of Engagement

Throughout my career I've discovered one principle of engagement that I believe has eluded most researchers. That principle is that <u>engagement is a progressive act. It's not an emotion, it's a series of progressive steps that are simple, straightforward and very predictable.</u> Yes, highly engaged people typically exhibit stronger emotions, discretionary effort and personal commitment but that's not how they get started. They start out just like everyone else, at the beginning of a pursuit with low awareness and understanding.

<u>The most important factor in the progression of engagement is that if you enjoy a game, hobby or career, you'll play it and spend more time in the pursuit of mastering it. The more time you commit to the pursuit the more you are likely to improve your ability and performance and become more engaged.</u>

The opposite is also true; if you don't like a game, hobby, or career you won't put forth the effort or commitment to mastering it. Every day people walk away and quit sports, hobbies, careers, and other pursuits that they no longer gives them a feeling of purpose, meaning, or a sense of accomplishment

They may be labeled as low or not engaged but my guess is that if you map their progress you can easily see where they stopped in their progression and predictability—when they became less interested and excited about the pursuit.

People don't start out good at new games, hobbies or careers, they get become good over time. The more they improve, the greater their understanding and proficiency and more likely they are to continue to improve their knowledge, ability, have more fun, experience growth, and begin to identify with the pursuit.

This progression of engagement is in every facet of our lives but for right now let's just focus on career pursuits. When a person lands the "perfect job," they're all in. They're excited to learn everything they can about the company, its products, and the industry. It gets better when they meet like-minded individuals who chose to start their careers with the same company.

They get even more excited when they meet those customers who are big fans of the company and their products. Could there ever be an end to the fun, personal growth and excitement?

As the employees grow in their abilities the "playground" rewards and recognizes them for seeking new challenges and learning new skills. Expanded responsibilities, titles and money are the natural rewards of achievement and progress.

Over time careers plateau with fewer opportunities for challenges and growth, which served as the fuel for their desire and commitment up to this point. These career realities are predictable and are at the heart of why employees lose interest in their jobs and go from high potential to a performance risk.

The progression of engagement is the same process that individuals and teams are subject to when they're introduced to new products, services or process changes within a company. No one goes from low awareness to an advocate overnight.

When you step back and think about the steps in the process and where programs seem to fail, it makes sense because it explains where and why the breakdowns occurred.

Throughout our client campaigns we recognized this factor and knew we always needed to identify where employees were in their progression to design programs to help drive them to the next level of the adoption curve.

<u>The more we used the Progression of Engagement model with our clients the more we realized that it could be used to evaluate programs with low adoption rates or new programs being introduced to an organization.</u> The steps in the model are on the following page.

Progression of Engagement

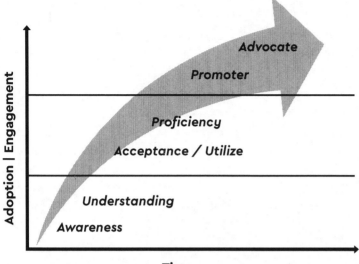

Time

Let's walk through the model to help you better understand it. For the sake of discussion let's use a launch of a new product in a company for the example. Your marketing department has designed a new product that they want the sales team to sell to your clients. Based on the research the sale is a no-brainer that your clients have been buying from your competitor for years. The challenge is that it's just not something your reps have ever sold or know anything about.

The marketing team designs a beautiful communication campaign for the sales team and a complementary training program to immerse them in the functionality of the products and customer needs. The sales reps attend the training and pass all the tests and give the instructor high marks on their knowledge and delivery.

If the sales reps accept the changes and utilize the tools and training frequently and consistently, the adoption rate goes up significantly. But if the training is not reinforced and the tools are not used the risk of no or partial adoption rates is even more significant.

By the way, this is where most programs fail to get adopted. It's your first red flag and where you need to build in feedback loops so you have an accurate gauge on your adoption rate. We'll talk more about feedback loops later in the book, but these can be as simple as activity trackers to monitor the number of sales calls being made by your team attempting to sell the product.

Proficiency is the next step in the process which can and should be measured as many ways as possible. I believe proficiency is the real tipping point in success of new programs and processes because it demonstrates a level of mastery that can provide sustained performance.

Moving from proficiency to promoter is based more on leadership than skills. Top performers, early adopters, and managers who have experienced early success can become positive role models and promoters. Promoters can serve as positive demonstrations of the benefits of the new process or products and can help reignite the energy behind the effort. Without Promoters it's difficult to market the change when no one is experiencing its benefit.

The highest level of adoption and engagement is the advocate. The difference between the promoter and the advocate is the head and the heart. The promoter is rational and the advocate is emotional. The promoter skillfully demonstrates the benefits of the new approach while the advocate enthusiastically encourages others to follow their lead.

The challenge with the advocate designation is that many self-proclaimed advocates are all hype and have never become proficient. When put to the test they quickly lose their credibility and the confidence of their teams.

Now think through how many times your company has launched new programs only to see them fizzle before they get widespread acceptance or utilization. Without an understanding of the progression of engagement model the company moves forward believing everyone is on board only to realize months and years later that their managers and employees never adopted the new concept and behavior thus limiting their improvement.

What I appreciate the most about the model is that it can clearly articulate where your people are in the progression of engagement with specific process changes, tools, and products. It strips the emotion of an engagement score out of the equation and can tell a leader or manager where their people are, why, and what needs to happen next to improve their chances of success and adoption.

Here's another quick example of how this can work. Let's say you've spent years and huge amounts of money to develop a new product. Your marketing team puts the final touches on the product and then rolls out the new product to the field sales team but after six months... no sales. You can go to the sales team and offer a new incentive or drop your price to the market, but are you sure that's the problem or solution?

By going back through the model, you can assess where the gap is occurring in the adoption and engagement process and focus your efforts in the area that will give you the best chance for success.

One recent project really drives home the value of this for me: My client had spent millions on new iPads and a special marketing application for the field sales force. They met with us because they wanted to look at strategies to help improve the adoption rate of the application and tool.

The adoption rate ranged from 50%–60% which was well below their expectations of 80–100%. The client thought the issue was with the design of their new application but also heard the iPads weren't reliable in client presentations. Since we weren't sure I asked to talk to field reps and managers to better understand the issue.

After an extensive study on the perceptions and utilization of the tools and application, we met with the client using the Progression of Engagement model to help them better understand where the field reps were in their level of adoption, what were the causes of the issue, and possible strategies to address the problem.

What we determined was that the adoption issue was the result of how the tool and application were launched to the field. Because the field sales team had a low understanding of the long-term potential of the technology, they never utilized the tools and never developed the proficiency to navigate the application successfully. They were stuck using the old outdated technology even though the new tool was much better.

The client thought everyone preferred the old system, but in truth no one knew enough about the new system to make the change. As we explored the reason why no one ever raised the issue earlier, we saw there were no feedback loops in the roll-out plan to flag the issue and gauge the adoption rate.

Having a disciplined step by step process and built in feedback loops are essential in helping leaders and teams set expectations, gauge progress and provide feedback and coaching on key areas for future improvements.

As we went deeper in the assessment, we saw the managers and leaders were as much to blame as the reps for the lack of adoption. None of the managers or leaders were using the tools or even knew how they worked.

The managers often reinforced the belief system and culture which prevented the new tools and application from ever being adopted by their teams.

When we were measuring the adoption rate by team it didn't take us long to determine who was responsible for adoption.

The field reps had a saying: "if it's not important to my first and second level manager it's not important to me." Tape that one to your door, your phone and your forehead!

The field reps gave great insight into their mindset because they knew better than anyone that their boss was king and—right or wrong—what he said mattered most because he made and enforced the rules. The key was making it their boss's priority which created the trickle-down effect on communication, expectations, and reinforcing the momentum of adoption as promoters and advocates.

Look out over the landscape of failed programs within your own company and group. Where do the wheels fall off? Is it in the awareness and understanding stages or the utilization and proficiency stages? Usually if people get good at a new skill or experience they become Promoters and Advocates.

The key is always breaking through those first two levels and getting your managers and employees utilizing and gaining a level of proficiency. Early successes reinforce the benefits of the change creating habit loops that create new beliefs and habits.

In a referral program we designed it was seeing customers installing products and services that Technicians had just referred to improve its promotability. There were even some instances where the process was so quick and effective that before the technician could leave the home the customer was talking to a sales rep and ordering the service.

Those were the stories we needed to get circulated and that's how we went from managing a program to the program going viral. Word of mouth among peers was more powerful than anything we could have written or said. That virility was how the program developed promoters and advocates overnight.

Seeing something work and work well is the ultimate advertising for your program. Knowing where you are and creating the right communication to drive your managers to each successive step in the progression is key to sustained engagement.

Middle Challenge questions...

✓ Where are your people on the Progression of Engagement model?

✓ Are your managers on board and do they understand their role in the process?

✓ Are managers leading their teams?

✓ Have any of your important initiatives been stalled and can you now identify where your people are in the progression?

✓ Do you notice a difference in adoption rates by coach and team?

✓ Do your communication, training, and recognition strategies drive the progression beyond awareness and understanding?

Bottom Line: Engagement isn't an emotion; it's a series of steps that we all take from low awareness to advocacy. Use the progression of engagement tool to identify where you and your team are and what you need to do next to become promoters and advocates.

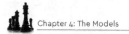

F = ma

The success of Moving the Middle is based on one simple physics principle that you learned in high school, <u>Force = mass x acceleration (F=ma).</u>

<u>Your growth (Force) is dependent on getting the most employees (mass) improving at the greatest rate possible (acceleration).</u>

Everything you do to improve the performance of your company and team should be centered around accelerating the speed of adoption of the greatest mass of people, your middle.

The graphs below are the same performance data presented in a different way to illustrate one simple principle. How you view and define a problem has a big influence on your approach to solving the problem.

The first graph is the traditional bell-shaped curve that most managers and executives refer to when they discuss strategies of Moving the Middle. When you look at the graph it's obvious "if we can get these average performers to behave more like the top performers our problems will all be solved." And you would be correct, but getting average people to be like top performers just isn't that easy.

I spent years in client meetings where managers would talk about improving the middle by training, recruiting, incentives and putting people on performance improvement plans to address the issue, but rarely did anything change.

After one client meeting a VP of sales pulled me aside and confessed the only way the middle performers were improving relative to the top performers was a result of so many top performers leaving the company.

The bar wasn't going up; it was going down and making the middle performers look like the top performers, but in truth they weren't Moving the Middle, they were lowering the bar.

When asked how he was making his numbers he said that no one was making their numbers and what we were seeing at the individual level was happening at the team and leadership level.

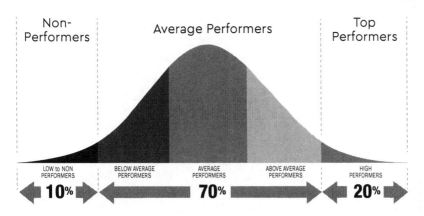

It was right about this time I was working on a customer referral initiative that had been operating about two years, and growth had completely stalled. The technicians that were active in the program were still submitting a lot of customer referrals but we weren't getting any new adoption and the numbers had gone flat. I kept thinking about that conversation with the sales VP realizing if revenue from the activity levels of the engaged technicians dropped off, the client would close it up and focus on other opportunities.

As I tinkered with the same ideas that everyone else uses to gin up excitement and production I put all the technician referrals in a quintile analysis and started to ask... what's the difference between the high performers and all others? <u>By looking at the problem with a new lens I was able to ask very different questions about what was driving performance.</u>

The chart below is an illustration of what a quintile analysis looks like.

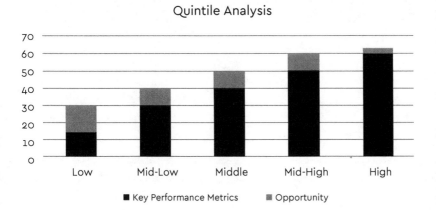

A quintile analysis is simply an even distribution of five equal groups or metrics. Let's say you have 100 people in your program that you want to analyze. Stack the low to high performers from left to right and for the value of each quintile take the average of each 20 individuals.

If your first 20 people on average are selling 12 widgets then the value for the low quintile would be 12. If the average for the low-mid is 30 then that becomes the value of that quintile. The variability in performance between the low and the mid-low would be 18. This process continues until you complete the analysis and have average values for each quintile.

As the variability increases from quintile to quintile it helps illustrate where your biggest opportunities are and where you need to focus your greatest efforts.

The key to the chart above using the quintile analysis is its ability to highlight the variability in performance from the top performers to the middle and low performers. You can use the quintile analysis to view sales, productivity, test scores and even referral revenue. The chart can also highlight metrics, business segments or people and help illustrate where you have the greatest opportunity for improvement.

One of the greatest benefits of the quintile analysis is that it allows you to overlay different metrics over each other to better understand their overall correlation to performance. The reason this is so important is that Top Performers in one area are not always Top Performers in all areas.

A perfect example of this was discovered when we were designing Five Star. Managers referred to different technicians and call center reps as their top performers but when we looked at the data we realized those individuals might only be the best in speed or sales but not in all the key areas of performance.

The technician who was strong in productivity might have low quality and low customer satisfaction while the technician that had lower productivity had perfect quality and high customer satisfaction. By changing the way we looked at the data we were better able to highlight individual strengths and need for improvement.

The technicians that were getting all the praise for how many jobs they completed in a day were soon being held accountable to the number of jobs that someone had to go back and fix and to their resulting lower customer satisfaction scores. The technicians who were more deliberate and did the job right and earned higher customer satisfaction scores were being recognized for their performance and contribution.

Another benefit of this approach was highlighted in the client's retail sales team when they realized that their reps with the highest sales revenue actually had lower customer satisfaction scores. By over-incentivizing their reps only based on sales revenue and not on customer satisfaction the customer experience was negatively impacted.

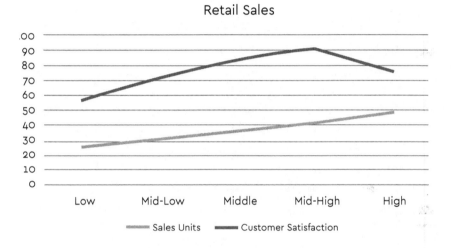

This realization would never have been identified or acknowledged by just grouping all the reps on a bell-shaped curve. The quintile analysis not only highlighted the variability in performance by metric but also by individual, manager and team.

Although it's important to understand the data on the graphs, it's more important to recognize that each quintile represented real people who were engaged or disengaged for various reasons. Understanding what's shaping those beliefs and attitudes is equally important.

One of the outcomes we discovered from the quintile analysis is that much of what we're looking at is an adoption curve. There are numerous reasons for the shape of the adoption curve that can be traced back to the

progression of engagement tool.

It's important to remember when analyzing data that the numbers are people and that people if properly motivated can and will change and improve. But no two situations are alike so it's important to understand and isolate factors and correlations such as tenure, training, experience, resources, and managers that might be the cause of the variability in performance.

In my experience, the greater the variability, the greater the challenge and opportunity for improvement. It's key to identify early on where the variability is greatest to understand where you should focus your time and energy. When you further break down the data by geography, teams, and individuals, you better understand what might be causing the variance and where you can make the greatest impact.

As you expand your assessment it's important to include elements like the experience of the managers, volume, and types of training, market conditions, regional competition, background, skills, experience, recognition, motivation, social influences, and other variables that can impact performance.

Take another cut and look at the data within the quintiles for trends. If different quintile groups have different trends, it reveals an entirely different set of challenges and opportunities as you determine what is causing the trend.

While the quintiles are critical to your assessment, it's equally important to understand the value of improvement. What is the value of a 1% lift by quintile? Where can you get that improvement and what will it take to sustain that performance?

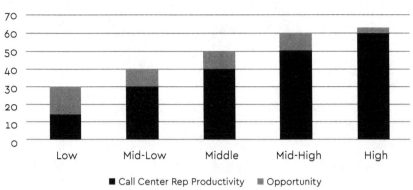

Quintile Analysis

■ Call Center Rep Productivity   ▩ Opportunity

As illustrated by the chart above, <u>it may be easier to get a lift from the top performers by offering an incentive but taking this approach limits the number of employees in the effort and minimizes the overall lift to the company.</u>

Over time, improving middle performers can contribute more to your growth curve and can sustain performance with less risk and variability.

Once you establish the baseline data for your organization, then look for those teams and individuals who seem to be defying the odds and breaking through the thresholds to the next level. This is key because they are in effect proving what is possible.

When you make plans to Move the Middle you have to put a fence around what group you are talking about and contrast that to your top and low performers. <u>By using the quintile analysis as a tool, you can quickly understand the variability in performance and determine the impact and value of the improvement by performance group.</u>

Focus is critical to success. Further intensify your focus by better understanding the key areas and people within your company that offer you the biggest opportunity for improvement.

<u>Everything you do to improve performance should be centered around accelerating the speed of adoption of the greatest mass of people.</u>

The middle has different levels of middle. Individuals and teams that are performing as high middle performers are very different than low middle performers which is why it's important to understand who is where and to design your strategies specifically around each group.

When we were operating the lead referral program we refined this approach by going out to the field, listening, and observing what was happening in the successful teams that wasn't happening in the teams with low participation.

As we analyzed the data we came across one piece of data that had massive implications to the long-term success of the program. It was the number five. When a technician or call center rep submitted five referrals it became a tipping point for performance. When five or more individuals on a team were active in submitting referrals, the program went viral and growth was explosive.

What we realized was that we were looking at an adoption curve and the key to our success was getting each individual and team over five. When people learn new skills, it takes repetition to get good and master the behavior. The key to our success was consistent and frequent positive reinforcement.

The technicians saw the referrals being done by their peers until they gathered up the confidence to do it themselves. They then went on to do it a series of times until they understood it, utilized the tools and gained a basic level of proficiency. After they did five referrals they might not be great, but they had overcome the biggest hurdle which was confidence.

These same individuals became promoters in time and went on to teach their peers how to do it. When five members on a team were active it created a buzz and the tipping point for the program to go viral resulting in over 80% participation.

If you want something to go viral in your company get people doing it and experiencing success, and you'll be amazed at how quickly their peers will adopt the new skills and behavior.

The key was to get the middle performers to do just enough for their performance to make it a habit and for them to experience the level of success and recognition that the early adopters were realizing.

Middle Challenge questions...

✓ How does the quintile analysis change your view of performance?

✓ What is the variability of performance between your groups?

✓ Where are your biggest areas of opportunity?

✓ What is the value of that improvement if sustained over time?

✓ What are the key elements holding back your middle? Knowledge, skills, experience, or motivation and desire?

✓ Who is the greatest opportunity for change?

✓ How does looking at the middle differently change your beliefs and attitudes?

 Bottom Line: The more we tested the theory the more we believed that what we were looking at wasn't a reflection of performance but of adoption. Those people on the far side of the chart weren't really better performers but early adopters with the right coaches, experience, and environment for the difference in performance. This is why the best teams have the most consistent performances.

Building Your Roadmap

What if you went to a surgeon with pain in your back and the surgeon looked you in the eye and said "my approach is simple, let's do surgery. I subscribe to the theory of ready- fire- aim."

How long do you think it would take for you to get out of that office and get a second opinion? How long will that surgeon stay in business? Why should your business be any different?

The surgeon uses a process or roadmap that takes him from identifying the problem, assessing the possible causes, and then designing a plan to test different medicines, surgery, or therapies to resolve the problem.

Building a roadmap that ensures you stay on track and reach your destination is a pretty basic concept, but you would be amazed at how many companies and managers launch programs with no process for planning at all! I am sharing this 7 step process with you because it's an extremely helpful tool to guide you through the design and launch of your program.

If you want to get the most from your investment of time and reading this book begin to take notes on what you've seen in your own experience. In previous attempts was there a focus on one group at the expense of the rest of the organization? What happened? How did it impact performance? Who responded and who didn't?

This is your opportunity to deconstruct your experiences and determine flaws in their designs and why they might have occurred. Was it a result of the bias of the leader, the company, or previous experience? How can you use this knowledge to improve the design and increase performance?

The performance improvement roadmap below is your guide to asking the right questions in your program's postmortem or helping you design a program with a fresh perspective.

Before getting started do you have an accurate definition of the problem and possible causes? If you have a problem with productivity then whose behavior needs to be addressed to improve performance?

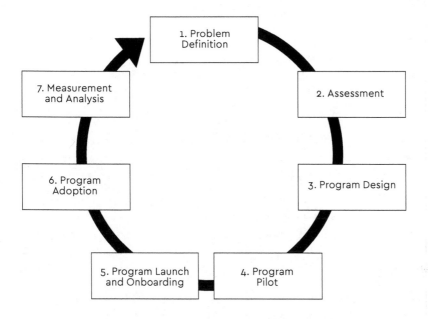

By the time you're done with these steps you're either amazed at the depth of the problem or swimming in data and trying to decide on what problem and area you want to focus first. That's an important decision because you can't design a program that will solve all your problems. Make sure you select the issues that have a ripple effect throughout the organization.

To get senior leadership support and buy-in we recommend the problem and opportunity framed as the "current state," the "desired state" and the "challenges." Agreement and consensus on what the problem is, its cause, and what needs to be addressed help in the next step of the process where you begin to discuss what needs to happen, by who, resources required, and how it will be implemented.

We all have an experience bias which is driven based on what we've been exposed to in our careers, cultures and our belief systems. Those experiences—good and bad—help us make quick decisions and get things done. However, there's a risk when the problem is more complex and you only address part of the issue without ever solving the real problem.

The assessment is the starting point for all your baselines, benchmarks, and business cases. There's a lot wrapped up in doing an honest and comprehensive assessment so create a plan, know what you need and don't start your design until you can confidently say: Ready-Aim-Fire!

When we were socializing the concepts with our client and getting Nos, we realized we were learning. Yes, we would have rather had a quick Yes but the Nos gave us the reasons why the concepts wouldn't work which was more important than a quick approval for moving ahead.

To overcome a No, you have to do your homework. The way we approached it was realizing that every one of these stakeholders is saying No for a reason, and unless we address that issue we are never going to get to a Yes.

What we learned through the assessment was that we knew more about the issue, causes and the culture than the leaders did when we finished. We did our homework and it opened the door to the Yeses because we created trust, respect, and credibility with our observations and insights.

The great thing about the assessment was that it built relationships with the field that gave us insights that no one else had. The managers and technicians liked us because they knew we were building the concepts from the ground floor up and not shoving another off the shelf program down their throats.

One such issue was the result of a new measurement system that was designed too quickly and to accurately provide feedback on the performance of thousands of technicians. To the client this was critical to their organization's transformation. The new system was ahead of its time in terms of scale, rigor, and functionality but not in terms of changing behaviors or delivering results.

Every morning the new system generated reports that were pushed to the manager's laptop and every day nothing changed. Well, that's not true. When one metric went down another went up. Just imagine having visibility to 73 new metrics and trying to control and improve them all at once. For the managers, it was like herding the proverbial kittens on a hardwood floor.

The system was rolled out to the field without any adoption strategy or sustainment plan and they quickly realized that all the reporting in the world wouldn't change performance. Data without insight is as worthless as plans that are never followed. They were swimming in data but no one had any idea how to make it actionable or how to use it to make the managers more effective and the field more productive.

To solve the problem the client quickly threw out an incentive plan called Pacesetters that cost the company millions and resulted in zero impact to performance. Productivity went up and then went down and the client quickly realized that they were in the same situation they were in before they launched the incentive. The question they faced then was should they offer more incentives to get productivity to go up or dissolve the program?

After a year of operating the program and the loss of millions of dollars in incentives, the client chose to discontinue the program. <u>It was painful and an expensive lesson but reinforced our experience that one-dimensional solutions breed bigger problems than they were designed to solve.</u>

After we completed an analysis of the problem and went through a design process as outlined above, the client agreed to pilot the concept called Five Star with 2,000 technicians and managers. The pilot not only demonstrated significant behavioral changes but resulted in saving the client over $500 million in productivity improvements over an 8-year period.

Instead of rolling out the next employee program of the month step back and think through how integrating the programs can bring more interest and depth to your audience. How often will they need to be exposed to the message for it to become part of the fabric of the organization? More times than not an umbrella program that can link together different initiatives has a better chance of sustained success than an individual program trying to get noticed.

<u>Change is a demanding master that requires constant attention. It's easy to get new programs started but experience shows that the challenge is getting managers and employees to see the benefit and adopt the changes.</u>

The larger your employee population, the more difficult it is to get these changes embedded in your culture which is why testing and piloting these initiatives with smaller groups increases your likelihood of success.

Engaging the middle is more complex than most people understand. If the middle isn't engaged emotionally and if those emotions aren't reinforced over time you'll be forced to launch a similar initiative next year because this one didn't work.

The ability to rewire your culture or mindset is at the core of sustaining the changes and instituting new beliefs, behaviors, and habits that will drive better outcomes. <u>The integration of multiple disciplines is where the magic is experienced.</u>

I believe the best part of this discovery is that in most organizations you already have many of the assets and resources to implement the plan. But you need a new way of thinking about the resources required to solve it.

Below is the blueprint to lead you through the first 4 steps of the 7-Step Process. Your game plan can be as simple or complex as your business issues dictate. If you have a team of 5-10 people you probably don't need folks from finance, IT, and marketing involved in your strategy design, but don't let the size of the audience undermine the importance of incorporating many of the ideas in the book in your strategy. As the audience gets larger, you'll want to be more cognizant of building a broader team, knowledge base, and resources to craft the solution.

Building an integrated plan may take a little longer but by incorporating different elements like recognition, training, technology, aspirational goals, and communication, you can ensures its impact and long-term success.

To get started let's go back to the 7-step process and really get clarity around the problem. Here are the questions we started with and always came back to because they crystallized our team's thinking.

- What's the problem?
- Why is it a problem?
- Who is causing the problem?
- What's the impact of the problem?
- Whose behavior is causing the problem and what specifically needs to change?

The key to success before you leave this step is gaining consensus on what the problem is and its cause. If the mission is to build a new training program start with the what, why, who and anticipated impact to improve your likelihood of success. What I love most about the questions is that they can guide you throughout the design process by always bringing you and your team back to your larger purpose.

The next step in the process is the assessment. It's easy and natural in the speed of business to jump from identifying a problem to designing a solution, but don't do it. One of the biggest reasons programs fail is the lack of due diligence in understanding the root cause of a problem and its impact on performance.

The better you understand all the factors impacting performance the better your chance of designing a strategy that actually improves performance.

Here are some of the key elements to consider in your assessment…

- Audiences (Individuals, Teams, Managers, Geography)
- Performance Issues
- Key Performance Indicators and Metrics (Sales, Revenue, Productivity…)
- Performance Trends, Data, Correlations and Quintile Analysis (Performance, Tenure, Products…)
- Volumes and Values based on Units and Percentage Improvements
- Training (Offered, Completed, Skills Assessments)
- Incentives (Programs, Valuation, % Achieved, % Not Achieved, Earnings)
- Attitudinal feedback. (Customers, Role, Manager, Company)

If you have the time and resources and want to conduct a deeper assessment here are the list of questions we used to better understand the issue and opportunity:

Engagement

- What are current and proposed program/promotion goals?
- What level of achievement are we experiencing? Per program and over time?
- What methodology are we using to set meaningful goals that optimize outcomes? What should we be doing?
- What impact are achievers having on performance? Vs. non-achievers?
- What is the average earning for achievers? What % of my budget is being earned by whom?

- Are other factors, like tenure, driving performance and achievement?
- What % of participants have improvement goals (MTM) vs. top performer goals?

Performance

- What are the desired business/performance outcomes for the organization?
- What is the distribution of current performance?
- How do managers impact team performance?
- Is there a high degree of variability in lead indicators?
- Are segments of the audience contributing differently to performance improvement?
- Is there a tipping point when participants are likely to adopt behaviors and sustain performance?
- What are the relationships (correlations) between metrics? Does one metric drive another? Are metrics working against each other?
- What is the current performance level/trend? What are the goals for the organization during the program period?

Financial

- If we drive improvement in one metric, what is the value of that improvement?
- How is performance driving financial benefit? Vs. goal?
- What is the long term trend of performance, and what is the value of that improvement over time?
- What am I spending per unit of production? Is that expense improving over time?

- If we drive improvements across quintiles (move the middle), what is the financial benefit by segment and in total?

- If we drive financial impact, what % of benefit should be allocated to the program?

As you wrap up the assessment you should have a solid understanding of the problem, its causes, its impact, and the value to improving performance. The answer is always in the data so making this a critical step in your design will ensure you're focused on solving a problem and not just building a program.

Here's a quick story to drive home this point. Prior to signing up for the Ironman I was stuck in the middle doing half Ironman races. Despite my training and skills when I would race I would blow up and finish in around 6 hours. My friends were all coming in between 30–60 minutes faster in the same races even though in training we were very comparable.

One day my friend Gerry Halphen pulled me aside and asked to look at my training logs because he was confident he could fix my race performance. When he looked at my data he laughed saying I was doing enough training volume to do an Ironman, but it was what I was doing that was holding me back. Gerry's assessment of my training log revealed my issue and once he identified the problem he was able to address the core issue. He helped transform my performance and knocked 45 minutes off my race time!

We went from focusing on pace and distance to heart rate and watched my race times improve overnight. The assessment was the key! Despite working with other coaches no one really took the time to understand why my performance suffered on race day. If Gerry hadn't looked deeper into the numbers, would I have ever improved that much in such a short period of time? No! The answer was in the data as it is in so many areas of life.

The next step in the process is in designing your solution. The keys in the design are shifting from a one-dimensional deliverable to an integrated solution. The reason so many programs never deliver the needed impact or potential is the field doesn't have buy-in to the strategy or adopt the new behaviors. To gain that buy-in and adoption a multidimensional approach will dramatically improve your rate of success.

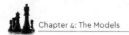

- Build a team from different disciplines of the company that have a vested interest in the success of the program.

- Try to get team members from Finance, Analytics, Operations, Sales, HR and Technology.

- Start the process by getting everyone on board with the research and problem definition.

- Get a commitment from the team and their leaders that they will serve and stay with the program until it's been launched. These initiatives take time and constant changes to the team can derail progress, trust, direction and momentum.

- Leverage the assistance of a senior leader for support and the use of a facilitator to lead the meetings.

- Concentration and progress are key to maintaining momentum and interest. If you can, do an offsite meeting of a day or two to begin the design. By doing so you'll greatly enhance your chances for building a plan that leverages the experience of the group.

- Success in the program's design is largely measured by the experience, buy-in and rate of adoption of the employee and manager.

- Do you have a strong emotional vs. rational why for participation and adoption? Are new skills required for success? If so, how will it be delivered, measured, and reinforced?

- If recognition is included are you using it to engage the middle or reinforce a top performer bias?

- How is the manager central to your strategy? Have you wrapped your plans around their onboarding and involvement?

Although it takes time and leadership is in a hurry for results my experience says to pilot everything, so you know how it will impact performance and behavior. Over 80% of the programs fail because the program owners don't understand the cause and effect of all the elements of their programs. It's easy to look back to understand why something doesn't work but it's much more difficult to anticipate all those issues before you launch.

Even if you just pilot your concept in a market or with your managers it'll give you a much better indication of your strengths and potential issues than if you go live overnight.

Build the pilot into your design strategy so you gain the benefit of the feedback from the users and the field. Just remember it's easier to tweak a pilot than to adjust a program that is struggling in the rollout.

Think Big – Start Small – Build Momentum

Middle Challenge questions...

✓ How many separate programs are currently in operation with your team?

✓ Which programs are successful and which ones have low adoption rates?

✓ Can you identify why this is the case and which programs can and should be integrated together?

✓ How do think this approach might help adoption and improve the viability of the program long term?

Bottom Line: The problem with middle performers is a complex problem which only gets worse when leaders take a one-dimensional approach to solving it. The life of your initiatives will only last as long and strong as your ability to integrate them with other initiatives and priorities.

CHAPTER 5

THE DESIGN

"Change is a demanding
master... but its rewards
are infinite."

– Jack Spartz

The Design

We were at our friend's house last week and talking about shows we love to watch. Everyone agreed that the HGTV "Home Makeover" series was the favorite. The show is about a family living in their parents' basement, for reasons unknown, that has outgrown the space and wants to buy a house way outside their price range.

A designer takes the family through the three worst homes in the area and makes them choose and pray that they'll be happy when the show is over and the camera crew leaves the property.

The show depends on the family not having a real option to buy a legitimate home, not having lived in a nice home, and being willing to be filmed when the story goes from bad to worse. For the benefit of the show's audience, all the bad stuff happens after the project gets started and the crew starts unearthing all the problems from the previous "fix it yourself" projects on the house.

The couple typically buys the house with the most potential and least cost giving the designer the greatest opportunity to show off and make it all look so easy.

After the couple celebrate getting the house for a better price than listed they show up for demolition day with family and friends. They knock down a wall here and cabinet there exposing the real issues with the house they just bought. $3,000 for the faulty plumbing, $10,000 to rewire the entire house, and $5,000 to fix a cracked foundation in the garage they've turned into an extra bedroom. Leaking pipes, mold, getting things up to code, and minimizing the risk of fires force the builders to realize that something has to give which adds to the intrigue of the show.

Somehow with all these issues and problems the house gets finished on the last possible day, right before their parents are kicking the family out of their basement. As the home is revealed for the TV audience and owners who haven't seen the house in weeks they are blown away with how the house is transformed. It makes for great TV because it makes the impossible possible.

What we don't see are all the people, all the hours, all the work, and the true costs that went into that one single project. It makes for great TV but if you've ever tried to do a "do it yourself" project outside of your skills, experience or understanding, you know you will be paying at least twice as much as you anticipated, take twice as long as it should have, and be left with a less-than-professional result.

Designing organizational culture, performance improvement and Move the Middle programs have a lot of similarities. There's a reason. On the surface, it looks easy and if you've read a few books, been in the workforce for a few years and have managed a few programs in your career you probably know just enough to lead the process.

It's not what you know but what you don't know that will be the reason for your program's limited success. The producers on HGTV focus on the designer but the real work and champions of the show are the plumbers, the electricians, the trim guys, and the carpenters. If they didn't use experts from each discipline their results wouldn't be good enough to keep you glued to your seat between commercials.

Now let me ask you: if your program design was being filmed and your project was being featured as must-see TV, how would it change your approach? Would you just trust your gut or really take a deep-dive to understand the issues and source of problems? Would you design the program by yourself or build a cross-functional team to leverage their skills, knowledge and experience?

If the camera crew were asking you to explain what you were doing and why you were doing it would you be able to respond with an intelligent answer that clearly maps out your plan or approach? Would your response reveal the real thought and preparation going into the design of the project?

When you have a chance to design programs like this you have an opportunity to make an impact well beyond the scope of your normal role and responsibilities. In my role with one client we were able to drive massive changes on a performance and cultural level, but it wasn't just one person designing the programs. We worked together as a team to assess the problem, analyze the data, and discuss possible design considerations and even ways to test our concepts.

The Team approach is why HGTV projects are so successful and why their shows are so entertaining. Your ability to lead a team of individuals outside the area of your expertise will not only increase your chance of success but will be an opportunity to learn and grow beyond your current experience.

My recommendation is to learn everything you can on how to plan, what to think about and the questions to consider as you design your program.

Use the questions in the book to challenge yourself and your team of experts to think about your design from different vantage points. There's a great line that says the better the questions the better the chance for success. Think of the questions in the book as coming from a friend or mentor wanting to make sure you consider every possible option before you move forward with your plan.

If possible, have your team members read the book before you begin your design so they understand the principles and can bring a higher level of thinking to the effort.

Middle Challenge questions...

✓ Who are the subject matter experts that should be on your team?

✓ What are the organizational disciplines that need to be included?

✓ What are the roles that you want your team to play to ensure a success?

✓ Who on the team has experience in leading an effort like this and what were their results?

✓ What can that leader teach you about the experience in your organization?

Bottom Line: Involving a project team of subject matter experts and answering the questions won't guarantee success, but getting their buy-in might help you reduce your chance of problems or failure.

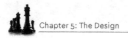

Integrating Training in Your Plans

I hope when you read this title it made you think... differently. The bigger the corporation the more available online training, which you would think is a positive until you see their results. Based on what I've seen in the past 15 years training has become so generic, ineffective, and sterile that it looks and feels like a microwave dinner from the 1970s.

I don't know what is behind the movement, but I'm sure it's another misguided effort to reduce costs and allow someone to make their bonus by slashing their budget.

If adoption and success in an individual's development is based on the steps in the Progression of Engagement (awareness, understanding, acceptance, utilization, and gaining proficiency) you would think this would be the one area that corporations were banking on to improve their performance. You would think. What I experienced firsthand was watching one of the largest companies in America develop and buy an entire library of online training to prepare its workforce for the needs of the future without any plan for adoption.

The CEO of this company literally held townhall meetings warning their employees that the company was going to be changing, the employees would need new skills, and that the training would be available through this online platform. It sounded good in theory but the problem with their approach was that there was no plan to identify the individual's needs, the required training and a plan to get there.

Sadly, the company isn't even aware of the situation because there were no plans or feedback loops put in place to measure adoption. They are not alone in this area. When training is something that's delivered by a separate department and success isn't measured based on its adoption, it's easy to measure success with the wrong lens, and everybody loses.

Leadership invested in the technology end up believing the field reps have what they need to be ready for the future. The managers are just trying to get their teams to do their jobs and make their quarterly numbers, and the employee that needs the training and guidance isn't getting it because there's no one in the organization who's responsible for their learning and development.

It's what I affectionately refer to as the illusion of training and learning!

A good example of this in the sports world is swimming. Swimming is a skill sport. It takes years to develop the right skills to become efficient in the water. A good swimmer can beat a good athlete every time because speed in the pool results from balance and skill, not energy.

Over the years it's been fun to watch 10-year-old kids show up at the pool and completely destroy athletes who have been swimming longer than the kids have been alive. The difference simply is that the kid with a few years of even basic instruction learns the skills to out-perform adults who have been swimming without that guidance and feedback.

The better the athlete, the bigger the ego which means the less chance they'll commit to learning the techniques to actually learn how to swim. I was one of those athletes and didn't come to this realization until I took a swim course called Total Immersion. I hated it! Progress was slow at first because they had to deconstruct my stroke and teach me the correct balance and technique. But over the course of one year I went from swimming 1.2 miles in 46 minutes to swimming the same distance in 32 minutes. I moved from the lower middle to the top in my age group.

The same improvement happened with everyone that took the training. We had athletes go from the slow lane to the fast lane as the result of the right process and reinforcement. <u>Yes, watching a video on YouTube would have been easier, more cost efficient, and given the illusion of understanding but in reality, it was clear that having a plan, a committed coach, and surrounding myself with good swimmers delivered the best results.</u>

Think back on your last training.

✓ How much of it do you remember?

✓ How much of it was implemented in your routines?

✓ Did it make you better?

✓ Was it self-directed or was it company issued?

✓ How was success measured?

✓ Was there a definitive ROI for the investment of time, budget and resources?

Now take that same list of questions and answer it about your team, division or company.

The truth is that most training is forgotten in a matter of weeks and months if it's not tested, applied, and repeated multiple times over the course of months. The "I watched the video and understand the material" result is as fleeting as the taste of a donut on the way into work. By not creating rigor in the discipline of training, companies are advancing without the bulk of their employees truly understanding the essence of their job responsibilities.

I have to admit that I've struggled with how training is delivered and success measured as they relate to Moving the Middle.

How are you measuring comprehension and skill development? By testing? Demonstration or results? What's the tipping point in training where the new skill is a habit that will impact results and outcomes?

Is manager-led training better than e-learning? Do the folks with doctorates know anything more than the managers in the field that craft the best practices and then share them by posting them on YouTube?

What I do believe is that if we retained and applied 1% of all the information we are exposed to in our lives we would be smarter and more successful than Albert Einstein.

How do you get your employees to remember and apply the skills, knowledge, and experience that can transform their performance and your business?

If you're going to develop and launch a new training program, before you sign off on the resource and expense think about integrating it into your bigger plans. If the training reinforces your communication campaign, links to the new measurements, and is reinforced in your company recognition then I think you're on the right path.

If not, you should be challenging yourself and your team on how this is going to be adopted by the field if it's not measured and reinforced. Reinforcement starts and ends with the manager. If it's not important enough for a manager to reinforce then it has little to no chance being adopted by the field.

Experience says to always focus training with your managers. If they become highly proficient and big promoters of the knowledge, skills or experience their people will be as well. If they don't, you shouldn't expect the field to be any different.

When my team designed training for the Five Star program it was always with the mindset that it would be delivered by the manager. The manager had an incredible span of control so we tried to make it easy to deliver, fun and experiential for their teams. Giving a manager training that they believed in and could deliver within a few minutes was one of the keys, but giving them reminders and tools for follow up and recognition of early wins was even more important in the strategy.

The importance of this approach is that the manager delivering the training becomes part of your integrated strategy, and over time the training, communication, measurement, and recognition become so well integrated that it doesn't feel like training.

If you feel you have all the training needed for your employees to be top performers change your lens and look at it from the eyes of your middle and low performers. Why should they be excited about the training? What about it is going to improve their environment, their status or their position within the team or organization?

✓ Will the training become a social experience where getting good or being the best is more about the team rather than individuals?

✓ Will you create meaning and significance at the team level that doesn't exist at the individual level?

✓ Will the training bring the team together to make it stronger?

Kids use elements of this approach every day to teach each other how to ride a bike or play a sport. When we train together for triathlons and Ironman races everyone improves together. It changes the dynamics of the group and creates a culture so powerful that it transcends an individual athlete's goals and objectives. The training we do together makes us all stronger and helps the middle improve well beyond their abilities.

Middle Challenge questions...

✓ Is your manager central to your training?

✓ Are your managers being held to the successful utilization and proficiency of the training?

✓ Is performance being measured and correlated back to the adoption of the training?

✓ How can training be utilized to build internal team champions?

✓ Who is delivering and owning the success of the training?

 Bottom Line: Measure training based on whatever, whoever and however you wish but having a deliberate plan, a committed coach, and a progressive model that gauges learning is the key to adoption.

The Importance of Alignment

One of my favorite questions from leaders: How do I align my organization so that the measurements down to the individual and team drive our top corporate priorities? It's a great question that highlights the importance of crafting jobs, roles and teams that are designed to support the company's goals. Think about it. How many employees on your team or in your company can describe how what they do impacts your company's goals?

In the realm of designing a program like Five Star, try getting 27 different organizations to agree on a set of consistent measures. It's not possible. We couldn't even get one division to agree on one set of metrics so we made one simple requirement going into the Five Star design meeting that became why we were so successful for so long. Alignment.

Just imagine that you roll out a new campaign targeting customer satisfaction. The company uses a very complex NPS (net promoter score) scoring system but you want to measure your customer service people based on direct customer comments and surveys not connected to the NPS system. Your employees are jazzed and getting great feedback from clients but leadership keeps watching the NPS score and it's not being impacted after a year.

If your leadership is like most, your programs will be shelved and something new will be launched the following year. The problem described above is why 80% of corporate initiatives fail to drive the anticipated return on investment.

If you can't measure something from the CEO down to the frontline employee it won't last long. The way I knew that our program would work in Five Star was because we tested it every possible way in pilots. The pilots helped us understand the importance of simplicity and consistency in performance measurement and feedback all the way up and down the chain of command.

The discipline became such a powerful force in our design that senior leaders used the daily field reports as their manager's scorecard. Despite having more reporting and drill-down capabilities than one could fathom, a one-page report that gave the status of their agreed-upon five key metrics was the basis for how they managed their business.

If you get the goals, key performance measures, and indicators right and you instill the organizational discipline to deliver the updates with the right frequency and accuracy, it's amazing how that one single effort aligns and strengthens the performance of the team.

The manager and frontline employee need to know those measures and how they are performing against them. If you add more than five to anyone's plate, they get the sense every day that they are playing whack-a-mole and are just treading water to survive another day.

When you get your progress measures right and get the focus on communicating, training, and recognizing achievement you can literally change your trajectory as a company. Every company and job are different so let me suggest five possible metrics that you might want to consider... safety, customer satisfaction, productivity, quality and efficiency.

The biggest reason for the alignment of the metrics is that it allows leadership to simply and clearly reinforce performance and progress in communications, training, and recognition. It focuses leadership on making sure that the organization is aligned and that employees understand how what they do matters. It unites the organization as a team and eliminates the case of winners and losers within a team. It makes everyone increasingly aware of the success and struggles that the company is facing which can become a great motivator to bring teams together.

When we faced the measurement and reporting issue in Just Ask, we faced the same challenges. The business group wanted to value the customer referrals for the lifetime value of the client, the consumer group wanted to get credit for six months, and marketing and finance wanted to only record the value of the actual revenue we were receiving from the referral. After considerable debate with everyone in the room we settled on a one-year annualized value so all referrals would be treated and valued the same.

It was the alignment and consistency of these measures agreed upon early on in the process that ensured its success despite changes in leadership and ongoing consolidations over time.

Middle Challenge questions...

✓ How are your team goals aligned with corporate goals?

✓ Does the team understand how what they do impacts the success of the company?

✓ Does leadership understand the front-line measures and how their success is impacted by their teams?

✓ Is there alignment on the goals and measures of success?

✓ Is leadership providing the tools to ensure progress tracking is being communicated at all levels of the organization?

Bottom Line: **If you get the goals, key performance measures, and indicators right and you instill the organizational discipline to deliver the updates with the right frequency and accuracy, it's amazing how that one single effort aligns and strengthens the performance of the team.**

Leaderboards, Dashboards and Scoreboards

When you walk on to a field where do you look to see how the game is going? The football stadium? Baseball? Games on TV?

Your eyes are naturally drawn to the scoreboard. We always want to know what's the score and how close the game is. Seconds later you start doing the calculations to see how big of a lead or gap your team has to maintain or make up to win.

The Dallas Cowboys Stadium boasted the largest scoreboard when it opened, and then the Atlanta Falcons created a scoreboard that's not only larger but because of its design has become the focal point of the stadium. The investment and technology are pretty amazing but what's even better is how it transforms the game experience.

It's amazing how we understand this principle in the field of athletics but don't use it in work. Are the scoreboards up in your business? If so what and who do they promote?

With the advances in technology it's easy to create dashboards and scoreboards at the individual, team and company level.

In Five Star we utilized a personalized dashboard that highlighted each individual's goals per metric and progress to date. If the individual was tracking to hit their goal the Star was lit up throughout the month. Every month a new set of goals were displayed on the dashboards, which highlighted whether they were improvement-over-self or best-in-class goals. At first the dashboards were updated weekly, but when we realized we could increase engagement by updating them daily we shifted to daily updates.

The managers got team based dashboards and could drill down on each performance metric to see who was above and below their goals. The dashboards became great tools for the managers and the technicians to discuss performance. The dashboards were operational all the way up to the president of the division which reinforced their use and understanding of the tools in the field.

When considering the use of dashboards, I believe they should be personalized to the individual in terms of how they are progressing and what that represents relative to their personal best.

The use of scoreboards on the other hand should be your tool for uniting your team together under common goals and mission. The team score is always an average of your team performance so sending out a stack ranking isn't necessary.

Everyone knows how well they are contributing to the score and if they are above or below the average. This in turn taps into personal pride and meaning rather than fear and public humiliation. Your team comes to work Monday morning like every professional sports team in the country… wanting to win and contribute. The effective use of scoreboards is a good way to unify their efforts. Why? Pride matters!

If your employee's competition is themselves and their goal is to beat what they did last week, month or quarter, now you have a real element of fairness, pride, and personal challenge. If their personal best and personal records are visible and something everyone acknowledges it creates pride in progress. How you celebrate success doesn't have to have a monetary value to provide social currency and personal pride.

People don't like to be compared to others, unless they're beating them. It gets old very quickly to always be compared to the top performers and the results can actually backfire on your plans.

If you do compare an individual to a lower performer, you might just be encouraging them not to improve and stay where they are.

When you compare an individual or team to themselves, you create a constant source of dynamic tension that is consistently applied.

Success leaves clues and the greatest motivation comes from the sense of pride when you know you beat the best version of yourself.

Creating programs that compare our performance to our best work is ingrained in our DNA, in our culture, and who we are.

If done properly, measuring someone's improvement against their personal best creates a positive culture of winning and expectations that may not cost you anything but the personal acknowledgment from their boss.

If you don't agree let me challenge you with the same situation. It's your team so every week your name shows up somewhere in the middle of a manager stack ranking that your boss sends out. If that really is the case how long have you been in the middle? Do you pay attention to it? Has it changed your performance or position on the team? There is always going to be someone in front of you and behind you if you're in an evenly matched race. The trick isn't to measure your performance against them but against your personal best.

It's not much different than measuring your company against your competition. Winning the battle and losing the war reminds us that a brief advantage against one competitor can actually set you up for a greater loss later on because you focus and measure yourself against the wrong things.

Teams win and lose together. Use the dynamics of the ballpark and team to pull your team together rather than have them take sides within the team.

Middle Challenge questions...

✓ What are your scoreboards?

✓ How often are they updated?

✓ Does everyone on the team believe they are connected with the results?

✓ How often is the team discussing strategies to improve their results?

✓ Are the scoreboards integrated with other initiatives? How?

 Bottom Line: The effective use of scoreboards is a good way to unify their efforts. Why? Pride matters!

Integrating the Experience

More than 20 years ago my mom received a pedometer for Christmas. It was designed to hang on her belt and when properly calibrated to give her the number of steps she was taking every day. It wasn't an easy task to get that little device set up properly but when we had it all ready she went to work every day in her normal routines and the device would tally her steps.

My mom worked as a volunteer in a consignment shop and was on her feet all day so she was walking a lot more than a normal Saturday or Sunday at home. She would ask if 3,000 steps was a good number and were 5,000 steps too many. Why did the device recognize more steps when she was out walking and fewer when she was working in the shop?

She would have loved the Fitbit. Easy to setup. Easy to understand, operate and to gauge progress. That heartrate monitor would have blown her away. She struggled with her health and fitness because of a bad car accident that crushed her back when she was in her early 50s. Knowing how many steps she was taking and being able to understand the relationship of that to her fitness level would have not only been engaging but would have been fun for her.

Up until Fitbit, the Internet of Things (IoT) was just hype. Fitbit to me was the first device that demonstrated to the average consumer the possibilities for integrating technology, personal goals, performance data, and delivering the information in an easy-to-use app.

Fitbit redefined the power of integrating activities, behaviors and results and as a result owned the market. It was featured as the hottest gift for years as they found new ways to enhance the experience.

The key to success in employee initiatives is fundamentally the same thing.

Integration.

Integration.

Integration.

Your employees are consumers and their expectations are driven by companies like Apple that have built their entire consumer strategy on integrating phones, cameras, calendars, email, and every possible application under the sun. Take a page from Apple as you design better tools to communicate, train, survey, provide performance updates, and recognize your employees while making it a seamless experience from the eyes of the employee and manager.

Create the experience from the eyes of the employee. When employees and managers start their day do they see how their team is doing on their scoreboard?

✓ Do they see their personal performance on their personalized dashboard?

✓ Does it flag them if they beat their goal or personal best?

✓ Is it reminding them how they compare to the team average?

✓ Does it have progress meters?

✓ Does it use social tools like messaging, where they can do the most good, when they're visualizing their performance?

✓ If something is off or the competition is rolling out new products or pricing, does the scoreboard have feedback tools to let your employees broadcast this knowledge?

✓ Does it measure skills training?

Put it all on the same platform, reinforce it and you'll likely get greater adoption levels!

If you have the metrics right and the technology integrated, it creates a seamless experience for the manager and front-line employee to monitor their progress. The integration of technology should incorporate communications, promotions, dashboards, scoreboards, training, achievement, and social recognition.

It doesn't have to happen overnight, but the vision should always be to create an employee experience that streamlines and simplifies all aspects of their communication, development and recognition so each can be used to reinforce the other.

When the technology for Five Star was at its best, we literally could launch and deliver a campaign to the field on a Monday with the communications, the training, the promotion, the goals, the progress tracking, and the incentives as one employee experience. That same experience would be adapted to the managers and leaders to ensure consistency and alignment.

When managing a program with over 60,000 employees, managers and leaders, technology can not only be a powerful enabler but it can dramatically reduce your expenses to launch and manage multiple campaigns.

When the technology advanced, we used it to get quicker completion of testing by using it as eligibility input for promotions. The technology even flagged individuals and managers towards the end of the month to show how close they were to earning a star based on their current level of performance and the goal.

Companies like Garmin are selling watches for $500 that Timex used to retail for $30. How are they doing it? They're integrating key performance metrics like speed, pace, heart rate, and cadence and delivering it to their consumers in an app that records, tracks, and even recognizes personal bests. Those same consumers are your employees, setting the bar for their technology experience.

Feedback loops in work are just as important when working with middle performers. Ignoring these individuals allows them to coast along at a pace well below expectations.

Knowing this to be true, why is it that so many people get to their annual reviews only to find out that they're not meeting expectations and only earning a passing grade for their efforts? Where were your feedback loops along the route encouraging, inspiring, and guiding their efforts? How did those conversations go? Was there an action plan that could have served as a road map to get them back on track?

Are your feedback loops built into your style as a manager and leader or are you waiting at the finish line each year to put the medals on the winners and fire the low performers? Don't laugh because if you're not regularly in the field talking to your team and providing feedback, you're missing the simplest and most impactful means of sustaining success for your team.

As you look back over the book and all of the ideas and suggestions on how to move the middle it's clear there are hundreds of combinations of ways to engage them on a higher level... but your feedback is most crucial.

Use the tools but commit to delivering the feedback personally. Walk down the hall, get in the car, and even pick up the phone— just have the

conversation and have it frequently with positive intent and you'll see the middle move right in front of your eyes.

When I got my first big job as VP of Client Services for a large direct marketing company I made it a point to be on a plane every week going to a different branch to be face to face with my teams. Anywhere from 8 to 30 people would be in the meeting room and we'd go around the room and give everyone a chance to talk and discuss how things were going.

The managers hated what it did to production that one day of the quarter, but the feedback sessions not only helped everyone in the division understand how we were doing, it also gave me a great opportunity to understand how we were doing. You see, feedback loops if honest and sincere can serve the leadership team in the same way they serve the front-line employee.

Automated feedback loops are designed for your team to help them be successful. They're tools for improving communication between a manager and their team.

Middle Challenge questions...

✓ How are you using technology to provide feedback loops for your employees?

✓ Is the feedback making a difference to the employee?

✓ Does the employee appreciate knowing how they're doing?

✓ Does the technology recognize personal bests and improvements?

✓ Are the feedback loops integrated with the managers' technology so they're aware of the improvement?

✓ How is this being reinforced to recognize the individuals/team and sustain the behavior and results?

 Bottom Line: Use the tools but commit to delivering the feedback personally. Walk down the hall, get in the car, and even pick up the phone— just have the conversation and have it frequently with positive intent and you'll see the middle move right in front of your eyes.

CHAPTER 6

THE FINAL CHAPTER

Why the Middle?

Your Customers

70% of your customer interactions and experiences are delivered by your Middle. How your employees feel is highly correlated with how your customers will feel.

Your Culture

The essence of your true culture is not that cleverly written mission or values statement but the attitudes, beliefs, and habits of your Middle performers.

The Economics

Achieve the greatest returns against the least expense.

The Physics

(F = ma): Force (growth) equals mass (70% of your people) times acceleration (rate of improvement).

Your Potential

The Middle is the greatest unrealized and untapped performance opportunity within your company.

Key Thoughts, Principles, and Bottom Lines

Introduction

- When we designed and implemented new initiatives we knew our success was predicated on changing deeply-rooted cultures and long-held beliefs and behaviors to improve results.

- You should expect you and your managers to be leading high-performing teams. That is an important distinction as you begin to understand how you can change the middle and the performance of your company.

Chapter 1 — The Mind of the Middle

- I began the process of underlining key passages in books and then copying them into my 5" x 8" notebook.

- This one extra step allowed me not only to have an incredible recall on principles, data, and research but by reviewing the material over time it helped me improve my understanding of experiences and events.

- If you're looking for a way to get smarter faster, start writing things down in a notebook and review it every few days. The physical process of writing things down crystallizes thoughts, strengthens your neural pathways, and helps you learn it, understand it, and make it your own.

- One of the keys to sustained success is baked in the principles of your employee's aspirational desire to do something extraordinary and be a part of a winning team or meaningful purpose.

- The middle wasn't an obstacle. It was a benefit because I learned lessons and established abilities that would have otherwise remained dormant.

- The key lesson about personal transformations and Moving the Middle isn't about skills or talent but hustle and effort. More times than not it's not a lack of skills that hold people back but their lack of desire to want to move forward.

- Lock in on that individual and hold on to that thought because as we build your plan and roadmap, it all comes down to creating the experience, one person at a time, that transforms your team and elevates your performance.

- The world, Ironman, your company, and your team are full of untapped potential just waiting to be inspired to sign up and do something amazing with their life.

- Most leaders don't have any idea how critical winning, desire, and motivation are to sustained success. If, after a period of attempts over time, your people don't experience success, they will lower their expectations or completely stop trying. They don't feel bad about being in the middle because the middle creates a culture all its own.

- Designing your plans and initiatives to highlight small wins fuels momentum, reinforces skill development, and creates an environment of success and winning.

- One of the keys to the Move the Middle approach is the power of small wins and the aggregation of marginal improvement and gains.

- Small wins are demonstrations of progress and achievements. With a clear understanding of all the key metrics, you can determine their correlation and relationship to progress and winning. I refer to these as trigger wins because each successive win triggers greater confidence, effort, and the next possible win.

- Small wins create a domino effect. When you knock one down, it can knock down a domino many times its size. Think of the power of that principle consistently applied to your business.

- One personal observation I want you to consider is that the key to Oprah's success is she didn't hire a manager to help her reach her goals. She hired a coach!

- Success is a progressive process and not a singular event.

- The difference between success and failure has more to do with your progress and position than your actual performance. Simply put, it's the effect of the Rubber Band or Dynamic Tension that controls your experience.

- So how do we disrupt this thinking and feeling of complacency? Successful leaders change the rules of the game by changing the perception of what matters and inspiring their teams to work together towards a common goal.

- One of our strongest influences is driven by those individuals in the closest proximity to our ability and performance. Understanding how this affects the perceptions of the middle is a critical step in the process.

- If you're comparing your middle performers to your top performers you're creating a toxic environment for everyone on the team.

- The adoption rates of their middle performers predicted success better than any other measure of performance.

- Every time the Middle spoke with their customers, their lack of confidence, motivation, and skills undermined every interaction. Instead of everyone becoming promoters, the employees became detractors.

- The beliefs of the team become the beliefs of the customers, which places an even greater emphasis on your focus on the middle and not just your top performers.

Chapter One Middle Challenge Questions

- ✓ Ask your middle performers to define their motivation beyond the paycheck.
- ✓ Ask why that motivation is important to them.
- ✓ Ask them when they feel their greatest sense of commitment and purpose.
- ✓ The better you understand their motivation the more effective you'll be in designing initiatives that connect with their goals and purpose.
- ✓ Start simple and build on your successes and learn from your failures. Consistency and repetition are the key.
- ✓ If asked, would your employees say they view their boss as a manager or coach?
- ✓ Does your leadership training reinforce the tactics of a manager or the role of a coach?
- ✓ Are there people in the middle who, if properly inspired and coached,

could become top performers?

✓ What are the mindsets of your middle and top performers?

✓ Are those mindsets positively or negatively affecting performance?

✓ Who are each of your teams' greatest influencers?

✓ Are they a positive or negative influence on behavior and performance?

✓ Are your programs designed to engage the middle or top performers?

✓ How can you use this knowledge to change the dynamics of the group and to reinforce the positive influencers?

Chapter 2 — The Manager and the Team

- To change our results, we have to believe that doing something different will lead to a different outcome.

- How you treat your people is determining how well they perform every day.

- By the way the fast guys were already finished with the race... these were the middle performers and with just a little bit of encouragement they came to life on the hardest part of the course. The more I cheered the happier they got, the stronger they felt the better they performed.

- The best coaches put the player at the center of the experience just like companies need to put the manager and employee at the center of their experience.

- When joined with a purpose, teams with strong middles beat teams with more talent every day.

- David Scobey, the president of the client I worked with, often said that "the best managers don't make their numbers based on a few top performers, but make sure that everyone on their team makes their numbers."

- People respond to managers and coaches that create a culture of winning and recognition.

- Making it about the technician rather than the manager transformed their relationship and took a middle performer to a consistent top performer.

- What happens between the concept, implementation and adoption of all these changes to improve performance? Why, despite the many investments in technology, does the middle stay in the middle? Why do the same issues that existed in human performance 30 years ago remain unchanged today? Could the answer be that leaders and managers today are more focused on the promise of technology rather than the adoption of new skills and value of personal improvement and performance?

- Where you spend your money is a neon sign for your values and priorities as a company. When training and development initiatives are cut in favor of the newest technology you are clearly communicating that importance and relevance to your people.

- Technology has advanced our ability to communicate, improve controls, and eliminated countless jobs but for all it's done, it rarely if ever improves the discretionary effort of your employees.

- Giving employees status motivation that comes from advancement creates social currency on the team and in their personal lives. When employees become specialists, experts or mentors because of their skill levels it signals to the world that they are being recognized for their leadership and contributions.

- The new strategy didn't last long because the top performer bias is so ingrained in managers' minds that many of the teams failed to adopt the real strategy behind motivating the middle.

- Getting and keeping your middle performers emotionally engaged long enough to change their beliefs and sustain improved performance requires new thinking, strategies and understanding of what drives behavior.

- You can't judge a person by what you see. It's what you don't see that matters. The dynamics of a positive group environment trump any data, skill, or experience you believe to be an effective means of gauging talent, ability, and potential.

- Creating winning teams rather than winning individuals is an important strategy because it transcends the rational motivation of the job by creating an emotional connection to the team.

- Where you are today is just a moment in time. How people are performing is just a reflection of how they've been treated, what they believe and how inspired they are about what they're doing.

- Behind all of man's greatest achievements is an aspirational goal and desire to be great or do great things. Tap into that force and you can move the world. Fail to ignite those aspirations and fail to realize your potential as a manager, a teacher, a parent and as a team member.

- The social influence from her environment, teams, colleagues, and family have an even greater impact on the outcomes than the goals themselves.

- Extensive clinical research has been done on the effect of social influences on individual behavior and it clearly points to the fact that we are products of our environment.

- The reason so many people do Ironman races isn't because it's something they've always wanted to do. Rather, it's the social influences of the group. The same holds true of the tattoos, the Ironman logoed clothes and car stickers.

- Promote the right social influences on the team and you'll naturally speed up the adoption rate of the right behaviors, beliefs, and attitudes.

- It's not what you do rather it's what you want your employees to aspire to that creates the best branding.

- Your employees are in effect your consumers and customers. If you want them to respond and build an affinity to your team and company, the employee brand has to evoke an emotional bond of trust, confidence, respect, inspiration, and aspiration.

Chapter Two Middle Challenge Questions

✓ What are your personal biases about the top, middle and low performers? Drive, skills, attitude, experience, knowledge, commitment, and contribution.

✓ Where did you get those beliefs?

✓ Do you treat different performance groups differently?

✓ If so, how and why?

✓ Who do you spend your time with at work? Low, middle, top?

✓ What kind of impact are you getting from your time and effort?

✓ How would your people say you add value to their performance?

✓ What are the seeds you've been planting?

✓ How have they affected your team's performance?

✓ If asked, what would your peers and employees say about your approach?

✓ Are there some obvious changes you need to make as a coach in terms of leading with a positive vision?

✓ What's your "Play Like A Champion Today" mantra?

✓ It all starts with you. Ask your team what their motivations are. Get below the surface answers until you hear answers that address family, career, and what's important to them.

✓ Listen. Employee satisfaction and engagement surveys are worthless. Go talk to your people. Word will get out if you're sincere in your desire to help.

✓ Take notes and show you care by making changes that address their goals and values.

✓ Share the feedback every time you meet with your team and employees. It shows you're listening and care about what was said.

✓ Do something small and build momentum.

✓ Whose (top, middle, bottom) performance will be impacted?

✓ What new skills or behavior are required to optimize the technology?

✓ What is the adoption rate in similar companies or industries?

✓ Who is really going to benefit from the new technology vs. who will be negatively be impacted by the new demands and requirements of the system?

✓ How is adoption measured and how does it impact performance?

✓ Start by throwing out your top performers. Create an unbiased assessment of your team without the benefit of the top performers. Force yourself to honestly assess your talent, future potential across all the key criteria for success.

✓ Now look at your middle performers and go through a "what if" strategy session and consider what if the top performers all left tomorrow... how would you begin.

✓ Where are your strengths?

✓ What are those weaknesses that can easily be addressed? Start with the managers. The change begins with getting them to understand that they are here to coach up their players, lead a team, and aren't there to manage people.

✓ Do you know the activities, behaviors, and experiences that are impacting your results? This is an imperative for you to develop and lead your managers because it's what they need to focus on in order to change performance.

✓ Is your middle skewed by individuals or teams?

✓ Is the middle environmental or attitudinal?

✓ Are there "events" that made the middle more defined?

✓ Is the middle created by social groups or norms?

✓ What are the goals of your programs?

✓ What's the success rate of your goals and that of your team?

✓ Are your individual and team goals aspirational or mandated goals handed down from corporate?

✓ How can you infuse your programs with positive social influences?

✓ What is your team's emotional commitment to their goals?

✓ Start with your current employee program branding. How many programs currently exist? When were they launched? What are people saying about it? How is it designed to make the middle feel?

✓ What's your history of success in employee programs? How long do they last? Why do you change them out?

✓ What is that aspirational desire that will become the golden thread of all your communications, training, and recognition?

✓ Are you wearing the shirt? Hat? Did you get the tattoo?

✓ How is the brand being reinforced?

✓ What would you like it to be and who on your team understands what you want and has experience marketing brands?

Chapter 3 — The Motivation

- You don't need surveys to find out which teams are unhappy and which ones don't want to leave at night. Your customers can tell as well, which is why it's so important to rethink the value in Moving the Middle in your organization. 60%–70% of all your transactions and interactions as a company are handled by your middle performers. Can you really afford to ignore this large of an employee population that services your customers?

- Goals that are devoid of emotion are devoid of potential and achievement.

- Improvement-Over-Self goals are the best at Moving the Middle because they create just the right amount of dynamic tension to keep employees engaged without making them stressed or demoralized.

- Believing goals are attainable is always the first step in achieving them.

- The first rule of motivation is that if it is not intrinsic, it will always require constant feeding and attention.

- To see something special in a person and inspire them is one of the most beautiful gifts of life.

- This ability to bring out the best in people is critical with motivation and the middle. Different performance groups respond to different stimuli and it's up to you to make sure you're giving each group the proper inspiration to maximize their motivation.

- The underlying thread for failure in corporate initiatives is the lack of motivation impacting engagement and adoption.

- Was there a strong WHY or HOW?

- The sum of your Behaviors + Activities + Results equals your Motivation. An easy way to remember this is: to raise the BAR on motivation measure your behaviors, activities and results.

- What we found was when offering cash as a form of incentive, the first two questions that most people ask are "how much is it?" and "is it worth it?"

- When you monetize the award value of achievement the calculative nature of your employees reinforces that it's more profitable to work a few hours overtime in a week than to be a high achiever.

- The biggest challenge when offering cash as the incentive is that cash becomes considered as part of the compensation package.

- Compensation is one thing you don't want to ever mix with inspiration. If you do, you devalue the intrinsic motivation which is the reason your team did it in the first place.

- Recognition is a powerful performance lever in driving performance and change in an organization. It signals significance, relevance, and shows appreciation in formal and informal settings. It creates positive press and a means for sharing stories. It provides a culture, atmosphere, and tools to show leaders and managers how to lead with a positive attitude.

- The same principles that motivate travelers worked with my client's employees when they changed from using cash incentives to points-based programs. By recognizing behaviors, activities, and results using points, the company could issue smaller increments more frequently to reinforce desired behavior while developing emotionally engaged employees.

- The new approach emphasized building equity in programs vs. cash based incentives to drive performance. As the equity in the programs increased, the client was able to reduce the value of the payouts while getting better results and greater participation.

- Motivation is all about aspiration and inspiration.

Chapter Three Middle Challenge Questions

✓ What are your performance levers?

✓ What are the costs of each lever and how does it impact performance?

✓ What are the levers being used the most and why?

✓ What are the levers that aren't being used but offer the greatest opportunity?

✓ How can you get expectations, training, and adoption of the lesser used levers?

✓ Who needs to be on your team to understand the issue and develop the plan?

✓ Are there any ways to pilot the use of self-selecting goals?

✓ Do you have data to look back at the success rates of different goal strategies, so you can learn from direct experience?

✓ Is there a way to test the different goal systems at the manager and team levels?

✓ How many individuals are achieving the goals?

✓ Is that an indication of progress and success or the lack of buy-in and motivation?

✓ Recognition is the positive **Reinforcement** for those activities, behaviors, and accomplishments aligned with the corporate values and goals.

✓ Instill leaders at all levels of the organization with the understanding that recognition (reinforcement) is the most powerful force in instilling a high-performance culture and leading a culture shift.

✓ Expand the reach, frequency, and tangible recognition (reinforcement) of employees and managers living the values, goals, behaviors, activities, and results.

✓ Celebrate and recognize (reinforce) those giving and receiving the recognition.

✓ Instill frequent, immediate, and genuine praise as routine to create a sustainable high-performing, high-touch culture.

✓ Establish baselines of engagement and performance to track, analyze, and monitor improvement areas

✓ Use employee recognition measurements as a barometer for engagement, attitude, and culture status.

✓ What types of currencies are using in your incentive programs?

✓ How are the awards being shared or discussed to create social currency?

✓ Is there any promotability to your awards to reinforce the winners?

✓ Are you using incentives as compensation or inspiration?

✓ Have you created a transactional or aspirational culture of recognition?

✓ How are you using compensation and incentives to drive different behaviors and results?

✓ What is your understanding of the impact this is having on results?

✓ What is working and what needs to be adjusted? Why?

Chapter 4 — The Models

- Engagement is a progressive act. It's not an emotion, it's a series of progressive steps that are simple, straightforward and very predictable.

- The most important factor in the progression of engagement is that if you enjoy a game, hobby or career, you'll play it and spend more time in the pursuit of mastering it. The more time you commit to the pursuit the more you are likely to improve your ability and performance and become more engaged.

- The more we used the Progression of Engagement model with our clients the more we realized that it could be used to evaluate programs with low adoption rates or new programs being introduced to an organization.

- The field reps had a saying: "if it's not important to my first and second level manager it's not important to me." Tape that one to your door, your phone and your forehead!

- The key was making it their boss's priority which created the trickle-down effect on communication, expectations, and reinforcing the momentum of adoption as promoters and advocates.

- Those were the stories we needed to get circulated and that's how we went from managing a program to the program going viral. Word of mouth among peers was more powerful than anything we could have written or said. That virility was how the program developed promoters and advocates overnight.

- Force = mass x acceleration (F=ma).

- Your growth (Force) is dependent on getting the most employees (mass) improving at the greatest rate possible (acceleration).

- By looking at the problem with a new lens I was able to ask very different questions about what was driving performance.

- One of the greatest benefits of the quintile analysis is that it allows you to overlay different metrics over each other to better understand their overall correlation to performance. The reason this is so important is that Top Performers in one area are not always Top Performers in all areas.

- It's important to remember when analyzing data that the numbers are people and that people if properly motivated can and will change and improve. But no two situations are alike so it's important to understand and isolate factors and correlations such as tenure, training, experience, resources, and managers that might be the cause of the variability in performance.

- In my experience, the greater the variability, the greater the challenge and opportunity for improvement. It's key to identify early on where the variability is greatest to understand where you should focus your time and energy.

- While the quintiles are critical to your assessment, it's equally important to understand the value of improvement. What is the value of a 1% lift by quintile?

- It may be easier to get a lift from the top performers by offering an incentive but taking this approach limits the number of employees in the effort and minimizes the overall lift to the company.

- By using the quintile analysis as a tool, you can quickly understand the variability in performance and determine the impact and value of the improvement by performance group.

- Everything you do to improve performance should be centered around accelerating the speed of adoption of the greatest mass of people.

- The key to our success was consistent and frequent positive reinforcement.

- If you want something to go viral in your company get people doing it and experiencing success, and you'll be amazed at how quickly their peers will adopt the new skills and behavior.

- It was painful and an expensive lesson but reinforced our experience that one-dimensional solutions breed bigger problems than they were designed to solve.

- Change is a demanding master that requires constant attention.

- It's easy to get new programs started but experience shows that the challenge is getting managers and employees to see the benefit and adopt the changes.

- The integration of multiple disciplines is where the magic is experienced.

Chapter Four Middle Challenge Questions

✓ Where are your people on the Progression of Engagement model?

✓ Are your managers on board and understand their role in the process?

✓ Are managers leading their teams?

✓ Have any of your important initiatives been stalled and can you now identify where your people are in the progression?

✓ Do you notice a difference in adoption rates by coach and team?

✓ Does your communication, training, and recognition strategies drive the progression beyond awareness and understanding?

✓ How does the quintile analysis change your view of performance?

✓ What is the variability of performance between your groups?

✓ Where are your biggest areas of opportunity?

✓ What is the value of that improvement if sustained over time?

✓ What are the key elements holding back your middle? Knowledge, skills, experience, or motivation and desire?

✓ Who is the greatest opportunity for change?

✓ How does looking at the middle differently change your beliefs and attitudes?

✓ How many separate programs are currently in operation with your team?

✓ Which programs are successful and which ones have low adoption rates?

✓ Can you identify why this is the case and what programs can and should be integrated together?

✓ How do think this approach might help adoption and improve the viability of the program long term?

Chapter 5 — The Design

- My recommendation is to learn everything you can on how to plan, what to think about and the questions to consider as you design your program.

- Use the questions in the book to challenge yourself and your team of experts to think about your design from different vantage points. There's a great line that says the better the questions the better the chance for success.

- Yes, watching a video on YouTube would have been easier, more cost efficient, and given the illusion of understanding but in reality, it was clear that having a plan, a committed coach, and surrounding myself with good swimmers delivered the best results.

- The truth is that most training is forgotten in a matter of weeks and months if it's not tested, applied, and repeated multiple times over the course of months.

- If you feel you have all the training needed for your employees to be top performers change your lens and look at it from the eyes of your middle and low performers. Why should they be excited about the training? What about it is going to improve their environment, their status or their position within the team or organization?

- The biggest reason for the alignment of the metrics is that it allows leadership to simply and clearly reinforce performance and progress in communications, training, and recognition. It focuses leadership on making sure that the organization is aligned and that employees understand how what they do matters. It unites the organization as a team and eliminates the case of winners and losers within a team. It makes everyone increasingly aware of the success and struggles that the company is facing which can become a great motivator to bring teams together.

- The effective use of scoreboards is a good way to unify their efforts. Why? Pride matters!

- If your employee's competition is themselves and their goal is to beat what they did last week, month or quarter, now you have a real element of fairness, pride, and personal challenge. If their personal best and personal records are visible and something everyone acknowledges it creates pride in progress. How you celebrate success doesn't have to have a monetary value to provide social currency and personal pride.

- Creating programs that compare our performance to our best work is ingrained in our DNA, in our culture, and who we are.

- If done properly, measuring someone's improvement against their personal best creates a positive culture of winning and expectations that may not cost you anything but the personal acknowledgment from their boss.

- Create the experience from the eyes of the employee. When employees and managers start their day do they see how their team is doing on their scoreboard?

- Put it all on the same platform, reinforce it and you'll likely get greater adoption levels!

- As you look back over the book and all of the ideas and suggestions on how to move the middle it's clear there are hundreds of combinations of ways to engage them on a higher level… but your feedback is most crucial.

- Automated feedback loops are designed for your team to help them be successful. They're tools for improving communication between a manager and their team.

Chapter Five Middle Challenge Questions

✓ Who are the subject matter experts that should be on your team?

✓ What are the organizational disciplines that need to be included?

✓ What are the roles that you want your team to play to ensure a success?

✓ Who on the team has experience in leading an effort like this and what were their results?

✓ What can that leader teach you about the experience in your organization?

✓ Is your manager central to your training?

✓ Are your managers being held to the successful utilization and proficiency of the training?

✓ Is performance being measured and correlated back to the adoption of the training?

✓ How can training be utilized to build internal team champions?

✓ Who is delivering and owning the success of the training?

✓ How are your team goals aligned with corporate goals?

✓ Does the team understand how what they do impacts the success of the company?

✓ Does leadership understand the front-line measures and how their success is impacted by their teams?

✓ Is their alignment on the goals and measures of success?

✓ Is leadership providing the tools to ensure progress tracking is being communicated at all levels of the organization?

✓ What are your scoreboards?

✓ How often are they updated?

✓ Does everyone on the team believe they are connected with the results?

✓ How often is the team discussing strategies to improve their results?

✓ Are the scoreboards integrated with other initiatives? How?

✓ How are you using technology to provide feedback loops for your employees?

✓ Is the feedback making a difference to the employee?

✓ Does the employee appreciate knowing how they're doing?

✓ Does the technology recognize personal bests and improvements?

✓ Is the feedback loops integrated with the managers technology so they're aware of the improvement?

✓ How is this being reinforced to recognize the individuals/team and sustain the behavior and results?

Closing

I hope this book challenged your thinking and exceeded your expectations by helping you realize the massive potential and untapped resources that already exist within your company—resources that are just waiting to be inspired and engaged. In most companies and for many of us Moving the Middle is a radical change in our beliefs and experiences, but once the middle is inspired and gains momentum it can become an incredible force to drive improvements.

I don't expect you or anyone to incorporate all of these ideas into your strategy for Moving the Middle but hope the ideas force you to think twice about your next big idea to change your culture.

Moving the Middle only requires you to think differently about your team and people in order to become the catalyst for great things to come. Start today and you'll amaze yourself on how you grow as a leader and coach.

I wish you the best and would love to hear from you as you progress on your journey. The torch has been passed... now it's your turn. All the best!

-Jack

Acknowledgements

The challenge of writing a book is only understood by those who begin the process, struggle with the complexity of the task, and then go on to finish the effort.

Throughout the process it would have been easy to give up, let go, and quit but I was blessed with some incredible family and friends that encouraged me to "keep writing" believing what they were reading would resonate with leaders, coaches and parents searching for the answer to how to motivate their middle performers.

Thank you to my parents who nurtured a love of reading, story-telling, and letter writing throughout my life. My Mom was a voracious reader who knew the power of knowledge and was always telling the kids with questions to "look it up." My Dad was a great writer, teacher and story teller. He had a beautiful way of crafting a story and left us with some great memories of characters and stories he made up on our family camping trips.

Thank you to my favorite authors who filled me with knowledge, experiences, and insights that transformed my thinking and life. Og Mandino, Dale Carnegie, and James Allen will always rank among my favorites and served as my mentors, coaches, and guides through my adult life.

Thank you to my brother Tom who challenged me to become a better writer and storyteller without worrying about the burden of success or results. Tom's nickname in college was the Guru, how appropriate. My favorite question from Tom was always, "as a result of the experience, what have you learned?"

Thank you to Justin Honaman, for your endless source of encouragement and inspiration. You not only got me started writing the book, but kept me going and made sure I finished. You are an amazing individual that has a profound influence on those you've touched with your enthusiastic belief and support.

Thank you to my siblings and family for encouraging me early on with my letter writing. All the letters I wrote you after Mom passed away and as Dad battled round after round of cancer were the only way I could deal with my grief in a positive way. Your notes back to me telling me I had struck a chord or that you had tears in your eyes gave me a sense that what I was doing was helping us all deal with the loss of our loved ones.

Thank you to my very good friend, Craig Hoffmann. Craig took the letters that I had been writing to my siblings after the passing of my Mom and created *Letters Home,* my first book, as a Christmas present. You saw something in my writing that would inspire others and planted the seed in my mind that this was possible.

Thank you to my best friend Bill Hague. Every ride with you always ended up being a best day ever. What I enjoyed most about our long rides were the conversations about work, family, and life. Thanks for carrying me the last 6 miles of Ironman Louisville. It will always be the Best Race Ever!

Special thanks to Mike Wien, Gerry Halphen, Meredith Atwood, Calvin Gray, Bill Spartz, Matt Spartz, and Jim Spartz for investing so much of themselves in reading the early drafts, providing feedback, and helping craft the story.

Thank you to Curtis Wall, Donna Stokely, April Ray, and Wanda Palmer for your vision, partnership and a friendship that helped create some of the greatest employee initiatives ever. I hope you know how much I admired and appreciated the way you treated our team. Curtis, you made us all better!

Thank you to David Scobey, Darrell Cooper, Dick Anderson, Rod Odom, Keith Cowan, Bill Smith, Tracy Garner and the many leaders throughout AT&T who supported, embraced, and led the cultural initiatives discussed in the book.

Thank you to my team members Adam Veazie, Bill Johnson, Matt Ellingson, Tina Nordsving, Jon Wagner, Julie Nelson, Lisa Miotti, and countless other members of the team that brought these wonderful initiatives to life. This was always a team effort and without your collective talents and experiences our successes would not have been possible. It was because of your creativity, hard work, and dedication that we were able to build a partnership that spanned over 16 years with one of the largest, most complex, and most demanding corporations in America.

Jack Spartz specializes in the strategy, design and implementation of performance improvement programs.

Jack is the 8th of 12 children. He is married and has 3 children, all graduates of Georgia Tech.

Jack was a caddy and was awarded the Chick Evans Scholarship to Indiana University.

Jack is a triathlete and five-time Ironman finisher. He has held sales, marketing, and leadership roles at Hershey Chocolate, Pepsi USA, US Surgical, ADVO, and BI Worldwide.

Moving the Middle NOTES

Moving the Middle NOTES

90887765R00115

Made in the USA
San Bernardino, CA
22 October 2018